PRAISE FOR
THE SELF-CENTERED PERSPECTIVE

"After having an opportunity to read *The Self-Centered Perspective* by Ray Stukes Jr., I am excited to apply the clear strategies laid out in the book towards his principal-based-living concepts.

"Working in the entertainment industry and telling stories sometimes allows for creative takes of one's own life situation. I hope by utilizing the strategies in *The Self-Centered Perspective*, I will be able to create more accountability around the decision-making process that I employ in my own life. I couldn't be more excited to put this life-strategy technique into practice."

—**Craig Chapman**, CEO East End Studios, Founder, The Solution Entertainment Group, LLC

"*The Self-Centered Perspective* is a refreshing and truly enlightening read. You cannot help but come away with an improved sense of self and a healthier, more hopeful outlook on living life."

—**Kristopher Heddings**, Father, Athlete, Businessman

"I am not typically a huge book reader, but this was one I felt compelled to keep reading with the turning of each page. It was such a relatable topic ,and I could see myself in much of the content, which gave me an overwhelming feeling of reassurance that some of the simplest practices in life can certainly lead to positive and sustainable change in the pursuit of a fulfilling life!

"As the author took me on a personal journey, he also created space to self-reflect throughout on my own life journey and all the things and experiences that have made me who I am and who I aim to be in the world. You don't have to be a book connoisseur to appreciate how well thought out this book is and how well it relates to just about anyone. No matter what age, ethnic background, profession, social status, it appeals to the human element we all possess, so there's a level of thought provocation that happens that I personally found to be extremely riveting and inspirational in my own quest in life!

"I have worked in Corporate America for over twenty-five years, been involved in coaching HS and youth athletes for over twenty years, and won multiple championships, and much of what I read has also resonated with these teams and reflected in the high level of success they've achieved.

"If you're a parent, share with your kids; a coach, share with your team; a boss or team member, share with your employees or coworkers, but this is an absolute must-read for anyone seeking the type of peace and fulfillment in life we often falsely think is impossible to obtain. This is the closest handbook outside of your own religious beliefs to guide you through how to successfully deal with real life! Absolutely loved it!!"

—**Tamika Daniel**, Corporate professional, Basketball Coach, Independent Filmmaker

"This book is a great reminder to take personal ownership of our individual lives by choosing to become who and what we want to be despite outside influence and common excuses. If we spend time improving, we can overcome life's constant challenges. I recommend this book to everyone!"

—**Chris J. Sheldon**, Attorney Partner Silver Law PLC

"Gratitude to Ray for confirming it is A-OK to be self-centered. The points Ray makes supports reaching self-actualization by highlighting a mindset of positive changes to implement a proper psychology mindset. Thank you for reminding us all to 'love being the only one of us running around in the world.' I am going write that on a Post-It and tell it to myself every day. *The Self-Centered Perspective* is a quick, fun read to put new pillar patterns of thought in the brain and body."

—**Noelle Hipke**, Award-Winning Best-Selling Author of *Superpowers*

"Ray Stukes Jr. has given us a profound new perspective on being 'self-centered'! Gone are the negative connotations surrounding being self-centered! Ray's message is clear: 'you must start seeing yourself as the messiah you are capable of becoming; whether the world knows it or not, it awaits your unique leadership.' This book is full of powerful, inspiring, and hopeful, thought-provoking messages to the reader! This book will evoke a sense of self-awareness, self-centeredness, self-validation, and balance! If you are ready to take control of your life and be your own hero, then this book is a must-read guide! The 'choice' has always been yours!"

—**Camille (Mia Bee) Benton**, Veteran and Entrepreneur, and **Traci (Traci Bee) Benton**, Mental Health Professional, Entrepreneur, and Singer

"Take a transformative journey through the pages of this enlightening book, where the author explores the complexities of self-reflection, the art of understanding one's self, and the critical task of navigating our emotions through life's challenges. This book serves as inspiration, prompting readers to discover not only who they are but also how to embrace a more compassionate and enlightened perspective on their life."

—**Laura H. Sexton**, Certified Paralegal

"I have known Ray for well over thirty-five years, and I've always been intrigued by his character, spirit, and demeanor. This book, *The Self-Centered Perspective,* explores the possibilities of what really lies deep within us if we have the courage to look. I considered myself a deep thinker, but Ray's examination of the human experience takes self-exploration to a whole new level. This book is deep and provides great insights and tools for managing your emotional state while grounded in a society which continues to push mental and spiritual warfare.

"Ray, I did not see this coming! I'm super proud of your accomplishment and deeply touched by your efforts to give back to humanity as a whole. Thank you for including me in your journey of life!"

—**Kenny Brown**, President and CEO, Nxmoov

"Wow! This book is fantastic! It came at just the right time for me! I am one that has been working on anger issues and just being a nicer, calmer version of me. A lot of what I have said or done in the past was done without any thought. I've had to dig deep and try to figure out why I did or said certain things. Some I have figured out, and others I have yet to learn. I'm still trying to learn who I am! This has helped me in the way it gave examples of HOW to go about things. Examples of things to say or actions to follow when I'm in my 'funk.'

"Other books or conversations with people tell me I should do this or that but never told me HOW! I need examples! You provided that! Thank you, finally!

"Also, my daughter was just here for Christmas. We had a situation where she expressed to me her disagreement with me 'always fixing my partner a plate.' My answer did bring up the love languages, but I wish I had gotten to the point of your book where you talked about doing things for your wife 'not out of gratitude or recognition or the expectation that it will be reciprocated' but out of pure LOVE. Those words summed it up perfectly, and at the time

I lacked the words to express it as simply and beautifully as you did. That being said, guess who I'm passing this book on to next?! Thank you. I can now practice to be a self-centered human!"

—**Vanessa Zebell**, Dental Hygienist

"*The Self-Centered Perspective* is a blueprint to transforming the negative into useful and productive activity, to become steady and in better control over our own minds. Don't keep it to yourself, but share it with others. We could all benefit from the knowledge it provides."

—**Cheryll Johnson**, Bookseller and Manager, Barnes & Noble

The Self-Centered Perspective: Using Self-Mastery, the Power of Introspection, and Choice to Balance Life's Ups and Downs
by Ray Stukes Jr.

© Copyright 2024 Ray Stukes Jr.

ISBN 979-8-88824-234-6

All rights reserved. No part of this publication may be reproduced, stored in a retrieval system, or transmitted in any form or by any means—electronic, mechanical, photocopy, recording, or any other—except for brief quotations in printed reviews, without the prior written permission of the author.

Published by

◄ köehlerbooks™

3705 Shore Drive
Virginia Beach, VA 23455
800-435-4811
www.koehlerbooks.com

THE SELF-CENTERED PERSPECTIVE

THE SELF-CENTERED PERSPECTIVE

Using Self-Mastery, the Power of Introspection, and Choice to Balance Life's Ups and Downs

RAY STUKES JR.

VIRGINIA BEACH
CAPE CHARLES

TABLE OF CONTENTS

INTRODUCTION 1
    Our Minds and Life Experiences 1
    The Impact of the Self-Centered Perspective 2
    Who Am I to Write a Book? 4

CHAPTER 1: WHAT IS THE SELF-CENTERED PERSPECTIVE? 7
    What It Means to Be a Self-Centered Individual 7
    The Origin of the Self-Centered Perspective 8

**CHAPTER 2 : THE FOUR-ASPECT PATH
TO SELF-CENTEREDNESS** 11
    What Is DNA? 12

CHAPTER 3: PERSPECTIVE 13
    What Is Perspective? 13
    Question Your Perspective 15
    The Origin of My Perspective 17

CHAPTER 4: UNDERSTANDING THE WAY OF THE WORLD 23
    Fair and Unfair 23
    What You Control and What You Don't 26
    Understand Your Game Plan 30
    Understand Your Purpose 30
    Understand Who You Are: Id, Ego, and Superego 32
        The Id 33
        The Superego 34
        The Ego 36
    Personality Assessment 37

CHAPTER 5: THE CHOICE IS YOURS 41
    Choose Your Traits 41
    Transform Your Traits 42

CHAPTER 6: THE FIRST PILLAR—HUMILITY, THE PILLAR OF UNDERSTANDING 45
What Is Humility? 45
The Balance of Pride 47
Hard Work 47
Natural Talent 48

CHAPTER 7: THE SECOND PILLAR—EFFICACY, THE PILLAR OF BELIEVING 51
What Is Efficacy? 51
The Best Teacher Is Experience 52
Vicarious Living With a Purpose 53
Be Down with OPP (Other People's Praise) 54
The Importance of Efficacy 55

CHAPTER 8: THE THIRD PILLAR—ACCOUNTABILITY, THE PILLAR OF INTROSPECTION 57
What Is Accountability? 57
Situational Accountability 58
Personal Accountability 61

CHAPTER 9: THE FOURTH PILLAR—RESILIENCE, THE PILLAR OF EFFORT, WILL, AND ACTION 63
What Is Resilience? 63
Mental Toughness 64

CHAPTER 10: THE FIFTH PILLAR—TRUST, THE ULTIMATE PILLAR 67
What Is Trust? 68
Trust and the Other Pillars 68
The Person in the Mirror 69

CHAPTER 11: NAVIGATING DIFFICULT INTERNAL LIFE EXPERIENCES 71
Navigating Negativity 71
Navigating Emotions 73
Navigating Stress 77
Acute Stress 78

    Chronic Stress 79
    Event-Based Stress 82
    Emotional Stress 83
  Navigating Loneliness 84
  Navigating Depression 87
    Clinical Depression 87
    Regular Depression 88
  Navigating Anger 90
  Navigating Fear 94
    Fear of Judgment 95
    Fear of Failure 98
    Tangible Fears 99
  Navigating Low Self-Esteem 100

CHAPTER 12: NAVIGATING DIFFICULT EXTERNAL LIFE EXPERIENCES 105

  The Tragedy of Death 105
  Navigating Illnesses and Disabilities 108
  Navigating Psychological Disorders 109
  Navigating Addiction 116
  Navigating Pressure 118
    Inner Pressure 118
    Peer Pressure 119
    Societal Pressure 120
  Navigating Success 122
  Navigating Relationships 124

CHAPTER 13: BE SELF-CENTERED 129

EPILOGUE 131

  The Logo 132
  Poems 133
    An Unconditional Relationship 134
    The Best Relationship 135
    A Message to My Wife 136

ACKNOWLEDGMENTS 137

INTRODUCTION

OUR MINDS AND LIFE EXPERIENCES

Although I disagree vehemently with many of Sigmund Freud's theories, there is one I believe in wholeheartedly: his theory suggesting the human psyche comprises three parts. Freud dubbed these parts the id, ego, and superego, which we will discuss later because they are essential to understanding who we are. These three components of the mind represent our emotional disposition and, in my opinion, are why we struggle to find balance when attempting to navigate the human condition.

The human condition is all-encompassing, defined by how our DNA, thoughts, perceptions, and actions respond to life's erratic nature. We must discover how to handle ourselves emotionally when dealing with vastly different stimuli, ranging from receiving tragic news about ourselves or a loved one to winning the lottery to our fourteen-year-old daughter declaring she is pregnant (hypothetically). In essence, the human condition is the story of our individual journey from birth to death.

Simply put, life is hard! No universal blueprint guarantees happiness and success for each of us. The human condition ensures we will face some of the same challenges and experiences, but we navigate them differently because we are not born with the same genetic code or foundation for learning. Similar life experiences include learning how to crawl, walk, and run, and how to talk, read, and write; developing skills to survive in the world; learning how to build relationships, how to get along with our parents and siblings, and how to make friends and find a life partner to love and to love us; determining our place in life; finding purpose for our life; discovering what it means to succeed and fail; and answering the question of the meaning of life. These are just a minuscule fraction of the unavoidable experiences we all deal with. Elements such as DNA and environment then add unique qualities; we have different physical features, talk differently, and even think differently.

Depending on our perspective, some of our experiences will be enjoyable, and some will be miserable. Either way, these experiences will profoundly impact our feelings about ourselves and the world. We humans must find a way to juggle complex emotions amid the chaos while keeping sight of what is most important. But how do we avoid getting lost on our life journey by focusing on the wrong things? How do we find the balance between drowning in a sea of depression, fear, and anger and flying too high based on genetics, overconfidence, good luck, and success?

The answer is to focus on ourselves more than anything else. Life offers many positive and negative extremes to keep us off balance. The best way to counter that imbalance is to keep ourselves centered.

◆ ◆ ◆

THE IMPACT OF THE SELF-CENTERED PERSPECTIVE

The next time someone says to you, "You are so self-centered," just smile and give a sincere thank-you. When they inevitably reply, "That's not a compliment!" smile again and say, "In fact, it's the ultimate compliment, and I appreciate you recognizing my personal growth."

From this point on, in this book, "self-centered" no longer means what we've been conditioned to believe. Self-centered now means to be comfortable and confident in our individuality and that our energy is focused on strengthening our character to maintain balance regardless of positive and negative feelings and events. This internal focus will allow our ideal selves to manifest out in the world, unwavering in our sense of self-worth and our belief in doing what is right for ourselves and others.

We will all experience ups and downs. It is impossible to manage life's challenges without something stable to anchor us. The main problem we face and the solution for that problem are the same—because we, us, people are the problem. The instability of our thoughts, emotions, and actions directly creates negative life experiences. By the same token, if we stabilize our emotions, we can ultimately stabilize our life.

The self-centered perspective is a way to strengthen our character by increasing emotional awareness and self-confidence to the point where life's ups and downs never throw us out of balance. We will be in control of ourselves in any situation because we understand that how we react is *our* choice. Understanding this is critical for the advancement of humanity itself. We have the power to usher in an age of understanding; the key to unlocking heaven on earth lies in the human mind.

Our perceptions and beliefs can influence every person we interact with. Positive influence leads to a domino effect. As those closest to us interact with their larger circle of people, and that circle influences overlapping circles and so on, positive interactions among people spread on a massive scale. Imagine people diligently working to improve themselves to increase emotional intelligence, understanding, self-acceptance, acceptance of others, and a disposition that encourages positive human interaction featuring trust and respect for all. The state of the world could improve overnight!

So, this is my message to you: you must start seeing yourself as the messiah you are capable of becoming; whether the world knows it or not, it awaits your unique leadership.

◆ ◆ ◆

WHO AM I TO WRITE A BOOK?

My name is Ray Stukes Jr. I will share a few of the relevant qualities and beliefs that contributed to my decision to author a book. I am a family-oriented person and a man of faith. I am a grateful son, brother, husband, uncle, cousin, and father of five. My family is what I cherish most in this world, and I wish them nothing but positive experiences. I figure if they adopt the self-centered perspective and you adopt the self-centered perspective, there is a much greater possibility for you and them to live a life free of fear, hate, paranoia, stress, and other factors that decrease quality of life.

With this book, I want to cultivate a more positive coexistence by showing how focusing on a personal journey to self-improvement will lead to more positive life experiences. The self-centered approach to life fosters understanding, respect, and appreciation for all individuals and their differences.

I obtained my college degree in psychology because I am fascinated by the power of our emotions, thoughts, and beliefs, and I wanted to expand my knowledge of the mind. I find it astounding that we can either accomplish almost any goal we set our sights on or self-destruct, all based on our thoughts and feelings. Having grown up as an athlete, I process life events through the filter of a competitor, and this approach pushes me to give my best effort in any challenge I face. This mindset was instrumental in taking on the challenge of writing a book.

I do not have a PhD or a long line of best-selling books. I don't have a Pulitzer, a Grammy, or an ESPY. You might be thinking, *No wonder this guy didn't want to give his bio. He hasn't done anything!* And that is precisely the thought process I'd like to reevaluate. This is, in fact, the first book I have ever written. Does this automatically disqualify me from writing a book? No, it does not, and here's why.

First, every best-selling author has a first book out there. Second, this book is about taking an introspective approach to the challenges of being human. My qualification is that I am a human being with forty-eight years of experience navigating the tumultuous terrain of the human condition. I am simply a person trying not to get sick on the roller coaster of life, just like you. Third, expressing my thoughts through a book has always been a goal of mine. We owe it to ourselves to do all we can to achieve our goals for personal fulfillment.

Lastly, and this is the most important, I have something to say about something I care about. I have found a way to live free of lingering negative emotions, and if it works for me, it might work for you. As I wish everyone a life with fewer emotional hardships, I feel compelled to share the enlightened state of emotional awareness I have experienced.

If Megan the mechanic writes a competent book about politics and Steven the secretary writes a book full of salient information on gardening, am I to discount the information based on who they are or what they do instead of analyzing the content of their work? One of my favorite movies is *Good Will Hunting*. If you are not familiar with this film, it follows a college-aged kid who has a reputation as kind of a hoodlum. He has had some run-ins with the law and works as a custodian at a prestigious school (MIT). Will is a genius, though you would not think so without getting to know him. Despite his rough-around-the-edges persona, he is every bit as capable as any student enrolled at MIT, if not more so.

You can't assess the depth or qualifications of a person by analyzing the surface. This is the kind of societal norm and traditionalist thinking I hope you will come to challenge as a self-centered individual. From a self-centered perspective, we are all qualified authors if we choose to be.

I hope my passion for introspective living will aid your focus on manifesting your ideal self through a self-centered perspective, thereby boosting your quality of life.

CHAPTER 1

WHAT IS THE SELF-CENTERED PERSPECTIVE?

> For what it's worth: It's never too late . . . to be whoever you want to be.
>
> —**Eric Roth,** *The Curious Case of Benjamin Button* (2008) Screenplay, Based on the Short Story by F. Scott Fitzgerald

WHAT IT MEANS TO BE A SELF-CENTERED INDIVIDUAL

Typically, when someone refers to another person as "self-centered," the term has an unfavorable connotation. "Self-centered" is synonymous with selfishness or self-serving behavior. Well, I am here to change that line of thinking. In my view, self-centeredness refers to a way of life in which an individual takes an internal approach to navigating every situation.

The self-centered perspective is rooted in a nuanced understanding of the traits necessary to survive or thrive in any setting. It means one must be emotionally balanced and able to think through situations with a clear purpose in mind. We must conduct ourselves in a manner that is self-sustaining to the point where adverse life circumstances—whether within or beyond our control—do not keep us down. The actions and words of other people can do us no harm. Validation from external sources is unnecessary to feel personally fulfilled. Most importantly, we understand our unique DNA has great value to humanity, and the only person qualified to put a price on that value is us.

Once we believe ourselves capable of emotional intelligence, we are struck with the realization that we have power when we strengthen our mind to work for us. We have the power to perpetuate harmony in stable situations or bring balance to situations in flux through our words and actions. When perspective originates from within, the focus is solely on what *we* can do in an active situation or what we could have done in situations that have already occurred. We never waste energy focusing on other people involved, what they did or did not do, or other uncontrollable variables. Self-centered people choose precisely who they want to be, and their perspective keeps their circumstances in balance despite external forces.

◆ ◆ ◆

THE ORIGIN OF THE SELF-CENTERED PERSPECTIVE

The catalyst in my creation of the self-centered perspective was a lovely woman from Maine. She is a passionate, hardworking, "pull yourself up by the bootstraps" kind of woman. Tough but sweet. Never misses sending a "Happy birthday" or "Happy holiday" to family and friends alike. Her name is Lois, and she happens to be my mother-in-law.

On her visit to our home in Arizona in the fall of 2013, she found a church to attend and invited us to join her one Sunday. I was familiar with church from childhood, but back then I was not there because I chose to be. I was there because my mom told me and my sister we were going, and there was no debate once Mom decided our plans for the day. Though I was physically there, my mind was focused on basketball, video games, and cartoons. I didn't pay much attention to the messages being delivered.

Attending church with my mother-in-law as an adult was a different story. Being far more mature at this point, I decided if I was going to attend church, I might as well try to learn something. I sat and listened intently to the pastor's message for that Sunday. I do not recall his exact words, but I remember how I felt and what I took from that sermon. I recall feeling as though the preacher were speaking directly to me, telling me it was time to take ownership of every aspect of my life. I knew taking ownership started with the way I thought about life.

That Sunday happened to be baptism Sunday, so the timing of our visit could not have been more perfect. My wife and I felt compelled to become baptized, and that experience changed my life. As I emerged from the water, it was RIP to the old me; a different version of myself left the church that day.

The message that came through was "Be present at all times because you never know when you will encounter a life-changing event." But the change in my perspective did not take place overnight. I continued to live my life and experience the same routine, only now through the lens of feeling reborn. I began to process information differently. At first, figuring out how to navigate life as a whole felt impossible because there are so many different aspects to it; still, I recognized that the common denominator in every life situation was me.

Then I remembered the three most valuable words ever spoken in a team sport: *Do your job*. We hear it over and over on the field and in meeting rooms. This basic, powerful phrase is telling you, "Don't look over there. Look in the mirror. Don't concern yourself with what anybody else is doing. Just worry about what you need to do. With any luck, everything else will take care of itself."

The key to life is that simple. If we figure out how to handle ourselves out in the world, life will change for the better. This message had become my mission. I created the self-centered perspective to guide how I conduct myself, and it has improved my quality of life immensely. Hopefully, it will benefit you as well. I am still on this journey, so hop on board; we are in this together.

Let's look at some critical steps that must be addressed on the way to becoming a self-centered individual.

CHAPTER 2

THE FOUR-ASPECT PATH TO SELF-CENTEREDNESS

> Understand: you are one of a kind. Your character traits are a kind of chemical mix that will never be repeated in history. There are ideas unique to you, a specific rhythm and perspective that are your strengths, not your weaknesses. You must not be afraid of your uniqueness and you must care less and less what people think of you.
>
> —Robert Greene

The path to self-centeredness involves focusing on aspects of life unique to us as individuals. What I call the "four-aspect path" encompasses DNA, perspective, understanding, and choices.

The most valuable commodity we have in this world is the fleshy vessel we see in the mirror. Nobody understands or cares as much about that reflection as we should, so that needs to be taken care of with laser-focused conscientiousness. Society, whether intentionally or unintentionally, manipulates us into thinking less of ourselves if we weren't born with an overwhelming talent, aesthetically pleasing physical features, or the ability to learn as quickly as others. We tend to compare ourselves to each other to establish our worth in society. As this will never be an apples-to-apples comparison, the exercise is a "fruitless" endeavor.

◆ ◆ ◆

WHAT IS DNA?

Our DNA is exclusive and separates us from the masses. That should hit us like a ton of bricks, considering how many people exist on earth. We are one in over eight billion. The value of our DNA cannot be measured by numbers and certainly not by comparison to another person. Instead, we should measure it by the effort we put into achieving the highest quality of life we can attain by carrying our specific genetic code on our specific journey through life.

We inherit some of our appearance, traits, and mannerisms from our great-grandparents, grandparents, and parents. However, our genetic predisposition does not mean we have a fixed life path. Certain aspects of our DNA are controllable. Traits can be learned, and each of us chooses the value we place on certain traits and the way they shape our personality. In many cases, even the appearance of our physical bodies comes down to choice. If an unhealthy physique or poor health runs in the family, we have the power to place more emphasis on diet and exercise to change that destiny.

We are responsible for carrying around our mind, body, and spirit. Finding a way to keep ourselves balanced in an unbalanced world is up to us, not our genetics.

CHAPTER 3

PERSPECTIVE

> The task is . . . not so much to see what no one has yet seen; but to think what nobody has yet thought, about that which everybody sees.
>
> —Arthur Schopenhauer

WHAT IS PERSPECTIVE?

In our daily life, we take in information, process it, and subsequently determine a course of action based on our interpretation of that information. Our days consist of a series of interactions with different people in different environments. These interactions determine our perspective. Perspective is the point of view we take when we analyze our life experiences.

When forming our perspective, it is important to ask ourselves how we feel about being human. Is it a blessing, a curse, or a little bit of both at times? If every person in the world answered this question, I believe there would be support for all three options. The differing responses highlight the effect of perspective.

Whatever our answer, perspective comes in at least three forms: optimistic, pessimistic, and realistic. All three provide value in certain situations, depending on which will serve our well-being the best.

An optimistic perspective sees life as a blessing, primarily focusing on faith, hope, and silver linings. A pure optimist would see only the good in people, places, and situations. This point of view can be helpful in terms of keeping a positive mindset in the face of an inevitable negative outcome. Optimism alleviates melancholy and prevents us from letting bad news keep us down, so our quality of life remains high.

A pessimistic approach sees life as a curse and always expects the worst in people, places, and situations. The primary focus is not on what could go wrong but on what will go wrong. Concepts such as faith, hope, good intentions, and silver linings provide little comfort. This constant negative outlook may seem unhealthy, but harnessed properly, it can be beneficial. Expecting the worst inspires us to put contingencies in place to deal with the fallout of displeasing outcomes. A pessimistic perspective can enhance preparation skills and provide peace of mind in tumultuous situations where stress might typically reside.

The realist perspective might say life is a blessing and a curse at times. It is the balanced or neutral point of view. There is no blind faith in positive outcomes. There is no needless stress over an outcome that has yet to occur; a realist carefully analyzes a situation where data might predict which outcome is more likely but will respond as they see fit after the outcome has transpired. The obvious benefit to this perspective is that emotions never get too far out of balance—never so high as to suffer a tremendous letdown and never so low as to suffer pointless stress and anxiety.

The way we see life directly correlates to the behaviors we exhibit while living it. We must identify the best perspective for our DNA and take ownership of our interaction with the world. This allows us to be true to our nature and heightens our quality of life. We must not let the world shape our perspective. We must shape our perspective internally to thrive in the world.

◆ ◆ ◆

QUESTION YOUR PERSPECTIVE

Perspective can be tricky. Allowing life to dictate what our perspective should be feels natural because our experiences so often shape the way we view situations. Somehow, we've managed thus far to journey through daily life guided by biology, secondhand information, and social norms that externally mold our perspective. But perspective should be based on aspirations of the type of person we wish to be and what we want to do with our lives.

Once we decide who we want to be, our perspective shifts to internal. Instead of allowing situations free rein over how we view the world, we take the time to analyze and ask questions—such as "How do I need to respond to this situation to reach a desired outcome?"

Too often, we allow our perspective of a situation to take shape based on the actions of other people or an emotional response. How many excuses and rationalizations for bad decisions have we made or heard others make? "They made me mad, so I . . . [insert regrettable action or retort here]"; "I was going through something that made me sad or stressed out, so I . . . [insert unhealthy coping mechanism here]"; "Well, his parents were sad, angry, narcissistic, drug addicts, so . . . [insert acceptance, pity, excuses, and enabling for poor decisions and reckless behavior based on environment and DNA]."

We tend to give ourselves and others a pass when we make poor decisions based on our emotional state, environment, or genetic predisposition. We often justify behaviors based on information we receive from questionable sources, such as entertainment, social media, or media in general. These outlets are notorious for glamorizing acts of aggression and destructive behavior because our brains are hardwired for negativity. We must be mindful and recognize when external forces attempt to mold our perspective regarding what is considered normal, acceptable, successful, meaningful, dangerous, trendy, or beautiful.

Raise your hand if you have ever heard this general life narrative depicting the American dream:

- Go to school. Get good grades.
- Go to college. Get good grades and obtain a degree.
- Get a high-paying job with that degree.
- Meet someone special, get married, and have two and a half kids.
- Buy a nice house with a white picket fence around the perimeter.
- Work until you're sixty-five, having raised your two and a half kids to be perfect, functional, productive members of society, and retire with your fantastic 401K plan from your awesome job.
- Travel the world with your spouse of forty years for the rest of your days, and gracefully pass away together in your sleep, holding hands.

Of course, there is a timeline for these milestones. If we haven't achieved them by a certain age, we are somehow failing at life. Sound familiar?

Do we ever take the time to ponder where these norms originated? Why is someone other than me trying to convince me what normal means in my life? Why is someone else defining what success looks like amid my unique circumstances? What part of that plan allows me to follow my passions and be genuinely happy? Where is the leeway for inevitable mistakes that will enable us to learn and grow? Where is the road map to guide us back from the depths of despair?

These are just some of the questions I asked myself at the beginning of my journey to self-centeredness, and I quickly realized the only person qualified to answer them was me. A strong personal perspective guides us to live with intent in a way uniquely beneficial to us yet indirectly beneficial for all humankind. It can lead to fulfillment we never thought possible.

You may be asking, "How can my perspective enhance not only my quality of life but also have a positive impact on everyone in the world?" The answer is two simple words: "understanding" and "choices." Once we make sense of the world around us and assess how we fit in, we can learn how to conduct ourselves in the manner that best supports what we see as our ideal self. When we start behaving like our ideal self, a self-centered person emerges into the world. We project an image other people will respect and want to emulate. And when people emulate our actions, real change happens on a global scale.

Over the course of this book, I share my perspective in hopes of uncomplicating life's challenges for you. Even if you do not share my perspective, it may help you develop your own, allowing you to live with a renewed sense of purpose, a reduction of negative aspects, and an influx of joy and satisfaction.

◆ ◆ ◆

THE ORIGIN OF MY PERSPECTIVE

The world can be complicated and confusing if we allow it to be. How can we find true happiness and joy in a place that produces more questions than answers, more chaos than order?

The process starts with making sense of the world around us. When we do not understand something, it is tough to act competently or have confidence that what we are doing is right. My journey to gaining perspective on the world began after my baptism, which led me to read the Bible. Now, before the nonbelievers start to moan, I am not suggesting that you need to share my perspective on faith to have a perspective of your own. However, I would encourage you to invest time reading the Bible as you would any other book, for learning and entertainment. It is a valuable source of wisdom on a number of different topics, and if nothing else, it will make you think!

If you're anything like me, you will find that Genesis, the first book of the Bible, can offer perspective on why our society is the way it is. My personal assertion is that God must be a research psychologist, and the world we live in is one giant experiment. Why do I believe that? Buckle up for my train of thought.

For starters, God created two human beings, Adam and Eve, equipped with unique brains capable of complex thoughts, emotions, and—the most dangerous powers of all—choice and free will. God understands that the brain hungers for knowledge and is compelled to follow curious impulses, and he wanted to find out what humans would do with free will. God's first test involved observing what Adam and Eve would do when given simple instructions. He provides the pair with a series of things to do and an explanation of what belongs to them (which is essentially everything!). There is only one warning, a single edict in which God says, "Do not eat from the tree of knowledge of good and evil." This edict includes the consequences for breaking this rule: they will die.

If I were Adam or Eve in this situation, the promise of death would probably be enough to dissuade me from breaking the rule—but, hey, different strokes, right? At any rate, despite having dominion over all things on earth except for one tree, Adam and Eve do not follow God's one rule, and they eat from the tree of knowledge of good and evil; apparently, they need to "have it all." That decision unleashes consequences on all of humanity for the rest of time.

Adam and Eve's inability to heed God's simple warning foreshadows how corrupt the mind can become when left to its own devices. The humans spawned by this disobedient pair make so many bad decisions and perform such unspeakable acts that God restarts the experiment with a great flood, wiping out all the participants, save Noah and his family, and giving humanity a new start.

Based on the decision made by Adam and Eve, God now has another question to consider concerning the human mind. "Do people give any thought to my guidance?" A weak mind can mean more than being disobedient. A warning is issued to the couple for their protection and the maintenance of their blissful lives, yet they choose to reject that recommendation, as is their right. This is a test of free will after all. What happens if God gives a command that should be rejected?

As the world becomes more populated and new characters catch the eye of the Lord, God administers one more extreme test of humanity relevant to my theory. God needs to observe the lengths to which a person will go in the name of loyalty, obedience, fear, or anything that inspires a strong emotional response. This test is administered to a man named Abraham, a devout follower of Christ, who is asked to prove his allegiance to God by sacrificing the only son born to him and his first wife.

To be perfectly transparent here, when I first read that, I had serious questions about God and why God would even request such a thing. It seems more like a request Satan would make. The crazy part is that Abraham was going to do it!

As I reflected on the fact that God did not allow Abraham to murder his son, it hit me. God never intended for a man who struggled for decades even to conceive a child with his wife to slay the child to prove his devotion. I believe God needed to know whether people would mindlessly follow commands from authority figures without consideration for right and wrong. A second form of a weak mind is one that is not capable of deciphering right from wrong on its own and relies solely on being told what to do by others. This is a dangerous quality of the human brain, and God knew it needed proper guidance and balance. Humanity needed someone to demonstrate how to use our tremendous power for thought.

For the experiment with humanity and the power of choice to thrive, God had to introduce a new variable: a cohort meant to establish balance. This cohort would influence some people to use free will more responsibly so the entire population would not fall back into chaos a second time. Enter Jesus. God's inside man showed humans how to live a life that is resolute, honest, humble, and free of negative mindsets. Jesus and his acts were and are to this day an example of how humans can use their power of choice and free will for good and positivity.

The conclusion in this scenario is either that humanity is capable of choosing to do what is right and good by overcoming the natural challenges that come with being human or that human beings are unable to overcome the challenges of being human despite the example Jesus gave and will always succumb to temptation and depravity. The experiment will not expire until the planet becomes uninhabitable. God cannot measure the results until the world ends.

And thus, my perspective on the world took form. Every human being is connected by our humanity first and foremost and secondly by our subjugation in God's grand experiment. We are all human subjects of a psychological trial conducted without our informed consent. We are being observed every time we need to decide on a course of action. If you've been searching for the meaning of life, there it is! Spike Lee told us what to do in 1989 with his movie *Do the Right Thing*. Jamie Lee Curtis, in the movie *Freaky Friday*, told us how to do it in 2003: "Make good choices." In my opinion, those two phrases define what we are supposed to do in life.

Now that we have this information, what do we do with it? This is where individual perspective becomes necessary in order to navigate the world on our terms. I believe the ups and downs of life have been predetermined by the choices and actions of the first two humans. I am subject to the same consequences Adam and Eve received because the punishment was for humanity, not just the individual transgressors. Of course, now that humanity numbers in the billions, the punishment feels a little steep! Nevertheless, that is my rationalization for events that do not seem logical. Why do good things happen to bad people? Why do bad things happen to good people? If there were true justice in the world—in other words, if being good exempted us from the consequences of Adam and Eve's decision—this would never be the case. But neither of those situations occur 100 percent of the time. No outcome is guaranteed. By that rationale, there is justice in the world.

None of us are immune to challenging circumstances. On the other hand, we all experience positive developments in our lives as well. So we have to choose which hypothesis we believe God went with. Does God believe in us? Or does God not believe in us? Understanding my nature, I view the world as though God hypothesized that human beings are unable to overcome the challenges of being human—even though I know that is not likely to be the case. I choose this manufactured motivation because I am the type of person who embraces overcoming challenges, and, most importantly, I do not like being told what I cannot accomplish. The more difficult the challenge, the more invested and motivated I become.

This perspective helps me find clarity in the unpredictability of life events. I believe it is necessary to have a solid explanation for the inexplicable. If my rationale makes as much sense to you as it does to me, perfect. That will help you through the toughest of times. If my rationale does not make sense to you, it is imperative to find a perspective that does. The perspective you choose does not have to be universally accepted; you just need to believe in it yourself. It will lay the foundation for understanding.

CHAPTER 4

UNDERSTANDING THE WAY OF THE WORLD

> The improvement of understanding is for two ends: first, our own increase of knowledge; secondly, to enable us to deliver that knowledge to others.
>
> —John Locke

When processing the chaos life throws at us, we must picture ourselves all alone in the eye of that storm. Ironically, that is exactly where we want to be. At times, these storms pop up with no warning and without provocation. Our very survival depends on finding the way out of disaster. If we can be the eye of the storm instead of a piece of debris or a bystander helplessly watching the destruction, we wield some power and control.

The eye of the storm is calm, offering a clear view of the events swirling around it. That perspective helps us make sense of life's random ups and downs.

◆ ◆ ◆

FAIR AND UNFAIR

The first aspect of "the way of the world" that we will examine from the eye of the storm is the notion of "fair versus unfair" as it pertains to being equitable. How often have you heard or uttered, "Life is not fair" or "That's not fair" when one person in a situation has a distinct advantage over the other? Probably too many to count. I believe the issue here is that people think of fairness as a remedy to the natural inequities we are born with. My assertion is that such a belief only weakens our fortitude and strengthens our sense of entitlement.

For some reason I cannot pinpoint, we have arrived at a point in history where "progress" is defined as everything being fair and equal. It's a nice thought in theory, but if all things were equal, there wouldn't be much diversity. The concept of fairness is an illusion.

Any situation where fairness comes into play involves people. And as we all know, people are not created equal. Equally valuable, yes; but equal? No. That is an undeniable truth, so no matter how hard we try to make a situation fair and equitable, it carries an inherent element of unfairness that comes down to human DNA. The countless variables comprising the makeup of an individual make it impossible for fairness to exist.

Taking the perspective that life is one big consequence of the actions the original two humans took, everything falls into more of a physics dynamic. Newton's third law of motion states, "For every action, there is an equal and opposite reaction." From a metaphorical point of view, this seems quite appropriate. To break down this theme, let's take a look at the key events that led us to a life of inequity:

1. Action: God grants humanity dominion over all living things and nature, apart from one tree with forbidden fruit.
2. Reaction: humanity could not withstand the temptation of tasting that forbidden fruit, so humanity fails God's test of self-restraint; in the eyes of God, that decision warranted a punishment equal to that of the transgression, so . . .
3. Action: God evicts humanity from the Garden of Eden and curses all of humanity to experience hard labor, pain, and death.

4. Reaction: humanity is forced to figure out how to survive a life mired in hardships and inequities as punishment for Adam and Eve's lapse in judgment.

As the above shows, life has been inherently unfair since the origin of man and woman. Adam and Eve made a poor choice, and we all have to suffer! I would be well within my human rights to question why I should suffer through hard labor, feel pain, and die. I didn't eat a forbidden fruit. I don't even know where the Garden of Eden is! That is certainly unfair, but that is the reality.

We entered this world with the same raw deal, so there is no reason to expect anything different down the line. We must not let the concept of fairness impact our thoughts or actions. After all, we have been dealing with unfair situations our whole life. Most of the time, fairness is invoked when the question is one of right and wrong rather than fair or unfair. If you still use the phrase "That's not fair," please stop it! It does not need stating. It should be implied and expected.

It is our responsibility to overcome situations where the odds are not in our favor. That is just a natural part of surviving this world. Besides, isn't it amazing how much "That's not fair" sounds like whining? I no longer see the world that way. I've accepted that the deck is stacked against me. Believing in fairness or that everything should be equal for everyone gives us a built-in reason not to adapt, persevere, and overcome situations that ultimately lead to character growth. Consequently, when external forces seemingly conspire to make situations unfair for us over and over again, we begin to believe we are cursed with bad luck and that a black cloud follows us around, sabotaging our lives at every possible turn. This black cloud becomes an excuse to become weighed down by trying situations and outcomes without giving our best effort to control what elements of that situation we can to improve our circumstances.

We must develop mental fortitude to combat this tendency and to traverse the unfair nature of the human condition.

WHAT YOU CONTROL AND WHAT YOU DON'T

The second aspect I consider a fundamental truth about life led me to develop a straightforward yet powerful philosophy. When considering the various scenarios we might encounter in our lifetime, one thing becomes painfully evident: we rarely control any of them! Outcomes are never guaranteed. We can engage in actions to influence a favorable outcome, but our hard work might still result in unfavorable results—especially regarding human interactions. Human behavior is the ultimate wild card. We do not control other people's behaviors, yet we must deal with them every day in some capacity. It is almost impossible to feel in control when dealing with the myriad personalities we encounter.

Once we realize how little of the world we control, our minds turn to what we do control. My list is concise: my choices and my actions. Upon that early discovery on my journey to self-centeredness, I developed a new outlook on how to function in the world. I am a simple person. I do not like unnecessary complications, and life already presents some big ones; I do not want to add more difficulty. So, every situation I encounter goes into one of those two categories. Either I have some control in a situation, or I have no control in a situation.

This simple philosophy changed my life forever. It is so easy to get caught up in what-ifs and maybes and in crafting contingencies to respond to potential outcomes. Before my epiphany, I lost sleep over stuff that hadn't even happened! That seems absurd when I think about it logically. I'll use driving as an analogy.

Every time I get in my car and drive, risk is involved. If I worried about all the potential negative occurrences on the road, I would become the personification of paranoia. Not only would I have to perfectly execute my driving to ensure my safety, but I would also worry about what every other motorist might be doing around me to sabotage my commute with their distracted driving—not to mention the other regular dangers such as traffic signs and lights; looking out for children, pedestrians, animals darting into the road, construction, debris; or rocks hitting my windshield. These are real-time worries and stress inducers to consider every time I actively operate a vehicle.

The more significant issue would start once my brain went off on a "What if this happens?" tangent regarding a blowout, a crash, or a breakdown. A breakdown could result in a crash. In the event of a crash, did I hurt anybody? If I hurt somebody, could I be arrested? Could I end up in jail? If I went to jail, my wife would probably take the kids and leave me. I'd probably lose my job. "Hey, boss, I can't make it in today because I'm in *prison*!" That call wouldn't go well. If I lost my job, I'd lose the house. And this would be my life. I would die alone, a divorced, jobless, homeless criminal.

As you can see, my train of thought in this example goes way off the rails and into a rabbit hole having nothing to do with driving. Even if I steered the train back on course, it would be met with more worry to navigate. What if I were hurt? What if I needed to go to the hospital? What would those bills cost? I can't afford hefty doctor bills right now. What about the car? What would repairs cost? Would I need a new car? Could I work? Would I lose my job if I couldn't work?

All that worry and anxiety blinds us to the tranquility of knowing we've done everything we can in a situation.

The practice of asking myself what I can and cannot control virtually eliminated all stress and anxiety for me. This simple situation analysis uses little time or energy. The beauty is that the process works the same for minor and major life events alike. In 100 percent of the situations we find ourselves in, we can simplify our lives by placing the variables into one of those two categories.

There is great comfort when dealing with events that fall under the elements I can control. If I am in control, all is well. If a task needs to get done and I am the one in charge of getting it done, I can rest easy because I know I will do whatever it takes to do so. There is also comfort in knowing that if the task does not get done, I know the culprit.

A situation outside my control may not be ideal, but it should still create a stress-free environment. There is nothing I can do, so my focus turns to controlling the only thing I always can: myself. I can sit back, relax, and wait for a tangible outcome to respond to; I can plan for different outcomes; or I can pray or hope for a positive outcome, depending on the nature of the situation I find myself in.

In the case of my driving example, the only elements I control are my actions on the road. All I can do is focus on getting from point A to point B safely through my own efforts. Why worry about what everyone else is doing? I have absolutely no control over the guy who had a "couple" of drinks and only lives a "couple" of blocks from the bar and decided he is sober enough to drive home; the teenager who has to respond to the most important text message in the world while rolling through a school zone; the guy who couldn't wait to eat lunch at his destination and spilled hot chili all over his clothes and lost focus; or the lady who decided to touch up that eye shadow in an intersection just before reaching the office.

These are examples of distracted driving that could impact any one of us anytime we are on the road. Instead of wasting valuable emotional resources being worried, stressed, or angry about other drivers, we should channel that energy into preparation and defensive driving.

The catch is we must be mindful of the situation and our emotions before putting the situation into a category and acting on that, which means being patient and processing all the data in order to make rational decisions. For the control freaks out there, this is probably a challenging concept to master because the purpose of everything you do is to be in control of a situation. If you take a second and consider the issue realistically, I believe you can understand how impossible it is to control every situation.

If we genuinely controlled everything in our lives, none of us would ever have problems because we wouldn't allow them to occur. Unfortunately, we do not always have control, and we may be unprepared for what comes next. But if you are a person who loves control, your preparation for adverse life events should be a stress reducer. If you have backup plans for your backup plans, you should worry less than your average human counterpart because you already know what your course of action will be if things do not turn out the way you would like in round one.

Now, what happens if something negative occurs that we did not account for? Heaven help us all in this case because here comes the full-blown freak-out!

Believe it or not, the best part of understanding the unpredictable nature of life is the realization that we do not have to be right when facing an unfamiliar situation that does not afford a lot of processing time, forces us to make a decision under pressure, and does not go our way. That situation merely becomes a learning opportunity. We might refer to this rumination as second-guessing, but that process is our brains trying to decipher how we could have avoided a negative outcome. A lot of us do this naturally; it's called reflecting.

When we replay a situation afterward, we often see where we could have done something different to increase our chances of a better result. By being objective in our analysis of our behavior, we grow and become better people. Mistakes are necessary for an individual to experience maximum growth. Trying to avoid them at all costs is futile, and being stressed or embarrassed by them puts us in a negative mental space. Mistakes can be valuable experiences for major success and more efficient planning in the future.

◆ ◆ ◆

UNDERSTAND YOUR GAME PLAN

Self-centeredness is a construct created to help us understand we are each the protagonist of our life story. We must believe ourselves to be the hero and behave accordingly.

We can probably all name a story with a likable main character whose principles we respect—who always seems to "do the right thing." In everyday life, things aren't so black and white. Recognizing the right thing isn't always easy. And sometimes that part is simple enough, but enacting the right thing is tricky, depending on the circumstances. How do we give ourselves the best chance to be a worthy protagonist in our true-life story? We must create a game plan to follow.

I am a huge fan of acronyms and acrostics, so I developed the HEART principles of life: the five pillars of being self-centered—humility, efficacy, accountability, resilience, and trust. Living with HEART is the game plan that will enhance our quality of life if executed correctly. These pillars will serve as the foundation for every action we take and word we speak and define who we are as people.

Mastering these five qualities provides a great opportunity to mitigate the stress we confront daily by providing emotional clarity when facing challenges. To achieve emotional clarity and walk the HEART path to self-centeredness, we must complete a vital task to squeeze every ounce of potential out of our personal growth: establishing a purpose.

◆ ◆ ◆

UNDERSTAND YOUR PURPOSE

Before beginning any journey, the most vital factors are the starting point and the destination. Without knowing where we are or where we are going, we are not on a journey; we are wandering and lost.

To decide the most effective path from the starting point to the destination, we must understand the obstacles standing in the way.

With regards to personal growth, that starting point is what we see in the mirror right now, and the destination is the manifestation of our ideal self. The most effective method to accomplish this task is to establish a purpose. It is always best to pick a purpose that is important to us; that way, we are more likely to stay engaged throughout the entire process. Someone once stated, "The two most important days in life are the day you were born and the day you discover why." Having a why provides access to an infinite amount of motivation.

I submit there is no worthier purpose in life, no greater "why," than transforming our mind into a self-sustaining, emotionally intelligent, self-centered work of art. Psychologist Abraham Maslow proposed that all humans strive to attain what he called self-actualization—reaching one's full potential as a human. That sounds like a lofty purpose and, quite frankly, unattainable by my interpretation. To attain one's full potential as a human is to be Jesus-like or perfect.

However, lying just beneath self-actualization, self-centeredness is an attainable measure of self because it's not about reaching our *full* potential as humans; it's about understanding our imperfections as humans and consistently doing our best to overcome them. Even our best will not always result in a healthy state of mind and perfect behavior. The focus in self-centeredness is on striving to strengthen our disposition and recognizing that overcoming challenges is a lifelong process not measured by discrete success or failures but by what we learn from those events.

By understanding the flawed nature of people, we also understand that finding our purpose in family members, mentors, or idols is a risk. Living exclusively for others or like others is not always in our best interest. People can let us down; they succumb to human nature and behave in ways that contradict our values. Even if the transgression is unintentional, the result is the same. We retain a shaky foundation for our purpose. The only one we can trust to have our best interest in mind all the time, in every situation, is ourselves. There should be no greater purpose in life than strengthening our character and emotional intelligence in a way that gives us the ability to function with certainty in this world of uncertainty.

With a purpose established, we can now analyze the raw materials we are working with to transform who we are today into who we want to be.

◆ ◆ ◆

UNDERSTAND WHO YOU ARE: ID, EGO, AND SUPEREGO

When we decide to live a life guided by choice, we must first understand who we are in our current state. In the first chapter, I mentioned Sigmund Freud's psychoanalytic theory, featuring three elements of our mind and personality: the id, ego, and superego. A royal rumble takes place between the id and the superego for control of the ego. Let me explain how this mental battle for supremacy defines who we are naturally.

Freud's theory breaks down like this. We project our ego onto the world. The way we look, dress, and interact with the world paints the picture of how we see ourselves and how others perceive us. When we look in the mirror after a long day, ruminating over the outcomes of everything we did and said and assessing whether the person we sent out into the world to take on the numerous challenges of navigating life was up for the task, we are reflecting on our ego.

The ego ultimately chooses every decision we make; however, the ego can be heavily influenced by the id or superego. Sometimes the choices we make are dictated by the situation we face, so how we decide on which version of ourselves to send into the world every day is where the magic happens.

When I think about the id, ego, and superego, I picture myself in the middle, representing the ego, while the id sits on my left shoulder dressed in a devil costume and the superego perches on my right shoulder dressed as an angel. As humans, we have many flaws, some of which are biological. When it comes to the three elements of the mind that make up our biological disposition, there is no exception. In a perfect world, we would have an amicable fifty-fifty split between the id and superego, making us an ideal blend of solid morals, trustworthiness, understanding, kindness, intelligence, confidence, fun, and responsibility. Unfortunately, that model of human is scarce. Most of us are a little heavier on one end of the spectrum than the other. Some of us are id dominant, and some of us are superego dominant, and the imbalance creates emotional struggles when we are confronted with circumstances that challenge our area of strength or weakness.

Let's look at how the id and superego can influence who we are in different circumstances.

◆ THE ID

The id consists of pure passion and deep feelings, which is not always a bad thing. When we think about the feelings, activities, and behaviors we enjoy the most, the id exists at the center of where we find happiness. Conversely, when we are overwhelmed by stress, anxiety, and depression and feel helpless to overcome those difficult feelings, the id squats at the center of that disposition as well. The id can be amoral, belligerent, conceited, self-serving, loud, fun, and thrill seeking; or it can be timid, fearful, and exhibit low or no self-esteem at all. No matter which type of id we possess, id dominance has a major influence on our disposition.

The differing disposition of the id is not a concern. The concern with the id is the extreme nature of whichever disposition our id happens to embody. There is no filter in communication, emotions, impulses, or behaviors. When our id homes in on a life experience that will provide immediate gratification, that becomes its only focus. It lacks reason and intelligence and will have an extreme response to that stimulus.

For example, suppose we are driving in heavy traffic, on the verge of being late for an appointment, and we are cut off by another vehicle approaching a stoplight intersection, causing us to slam on the brakes, stop our momentum, and subsequently miss the light, thereby extending our commute. Our furious id immediately starts talking retaliation: "We have got to catch up to this guy and cut him off in return. Eye for an eye! No. We need to rear-end this guy, show him actions have consequences! No, run him off the road altogether. Guys like this don't deserve to commute with the rest of us! Better yet, let's follow him to wherever he's going and slash all of his tires. That way we can make sure he's not on the road anytime soon!"

Of course, these are all unbelievably bad suggestions leading to a very negative outcome. Can you think of a more dangerous combination of qualities than a lack of intelligence, impulse control, and a filter paired with being extremely emotional? For those of us who live an id-dominant existence, emotional responses lead when facing challenges. This is not to imply that id-dominant people are inherently unintelligent; simply, an id-heavy personality is more likely to act and react to situations instinctively as opposed to using reason and intellect.

However, there is good news. The id may be dominant, but it is not alone. The very formidable superego can help balance out those impulses.

◆ THE SUPEREGO

Our mental guide for morals, ethics, and truth, all decked out in white, accessorizing with wings and a halo and always attempting to influence us to do what is right, the superego is the polar opposite of the id. The superego is about perfection and expectations. It is never wrong. It doesn't do mistakes. It is always proper, appropriate, logical, polite, protective, and respectful.

On the surface, these seem like qualities we should want to exhibit when interacting with the world, but there is an issue with the superego just as with the id. The id may be overly emotional and carry around potentially unhealthy baggage, but the superego tends toward too little emotion and feelings or none at all, which can cause problems when we need to show compassion or sympathy.

The superego can feel robotic in its approach to life, and that lessens the fun and excitement life has to offer. Its exacting nature and propensity to protect itself from all types of danger and negativity can cause issues in relationships. In a romantic relationship, an overactive superego encourages us to be perfect but also demands perfection from our partners. The superego cannot tolerate the inevitable flaws, which leads to constant criticisms, disappointment, dissatisfaction, and judgment of our partner's character. If we were only superego, no relationship would last.

Knowing that life is riddled with challenges and that we are likely to face failure at many different points, we must acknowledge that the superego is not helpful in these situations. The superego is likely to dissuade us from taking on challenges with long odds, to give up when a task requires several attempts before achieving success. Our superego cannot process failure or the feeling of incompetence. If you or someone you know has an external excuse for every failure, that is the superego protecting its notion of being perfect. Failure is never the fault of a superego-driven individual.

In short, the superego is a fixed mindset not built on resilience. That said, it is a necessary yin to the yang of the id. Without the superego, humanity would rage out of control and probably incite the biblical flood 2.0.

Returning to the traffic example, as the id rambles off impulsive, terrible ideas, the superego counters with altruistic, reasonable, and rational responses. Instead of payback, the superego might focus on the fact that there was no car accident and nobody was injured. Or it might justify the behavior of the reckless driver by manufacturing a reason: perhaps the driver is rushing to the hospital because someone in their family has been seriously injured, or maybe they are about to miss the birth of their first child. This makes the dangerous driving feel more acceptable. Even if we view the dangerous driving as an act of selfishness and total disregard for others on the road, the superego will not take the action personally but instead may decide to pray for that driver to find peace of mind and be more considerate so they do not endanger themselves or other drivers.

Nestled between the two opposite perspectives of the superego and the id, the ego is tasked with finding the middle ground and executing appropriate behaviors when interacting with the world.

◆ THE EGO

The ego, or the persona we present to the world, has a tough job balancing the other parts of our mind. The ego must sift through the myriad suggestions of the id and superego and decide a prudent course of action. In a situation such as the reckless driver cutting us off, the ego must find the middle ground between the id's emotional response and the superego's charitable one. The part of the mind we are more influenced by will determine the actual physical action we take.

An id-heavy personality might not go as far as slashing tires but instead decide to present the reckless driver with a hand gesture involving a specific finger to show disapproval. A superego-heavy personality might give a disapproving headshake or shrug it off altogether and move on with the day. Whichever action we decide on likely feels natural to us. Without our giving the situation conscious thought, the ego is influenced more heavily by either the id or the superego, and we accept our behavior as who we are. If we reflect on our behavior, we would discover that our reaction reflects how we behave in similar situations.

Understanding these three elements of the mind lays the foundation for understanding who we are because we have a clearer picture of where our influence is coming from. We can now examine our personality from the core to the surface, which is the next step in figuring out who we are right now.

◆ ◆ ◆

PERSONALITY ASSESSMENT

As we set out on our quest to become self-centered, an honest self-assessment is crucial. We typically define who we are by our DNA, dominant personality traits, what we do or have done successfully, and aspects of life we enjoy.

For example, a quick summation of who I am would be the following: Physically, I am a relatively average-sized male. I am an easygoing Taurus with a calm, understanding, and patient demeanor. I self-identify as a family man, a man of faith, and an athlete. I enjoy football, basketball, golf, music, movies, a little art, anime, Mountain Dew, and I love me some pancakes! In a nutshell, these elements represent the perception I have of myself.

When I was first looking to establish an identity rooted in core principles, however, I knew I needed to dig deeper. My first realization was that getting to know myself was more involved than I initially thought.

To select the traits I thought best described who I was, I asked myself generic, interview-type questions: What do you like about yourself? What do you dislike about yourself? What brings you joy? What inspires you? What makes you angry or sad? How do you handle stress, negativity, or confrontation? Do you enjoy the company of people? I soon discovered these questions could extend infinitely, so I switched gears and took the 16 Personalities online test. At the very least, I knew the questions would end at some point and be targeted enough to generate a personality type based on my responses.

In case you were wondering, I popped up as an INFP-A type. According to Myers and Briggs, this stands for introvert, intuitive, feeling, and perceiving. The "A" stands for assertive, which apparently is the rarer form of the INFP types. I agreed with the results and felt the personality test gave me a decent picture of how I saw myself, but the assessment seemed incomplete.

My second realization was how many different personality traits I could potentially possess as an INFP-A personality type. The number was overwhelming. It could have taken weeks to sort out which of the thousands of traits best described who I was then. The third realization I came to was how fickle certain traits are. I discovered that I might be jealous in one situation but not all situations. I could be a free spirit in one particular environment and conservative in another. The traits we display often contradict one another depending on circumstance.

Because traits are so situational, pinpointing which represented me best was difficult. Was I a jealous person or not? Was I free-spirited, or was I not? I decided if the answer was "Sometimes," that trait wasn't definitive enough to understand the type of person I was at the core. Another issue with my self-assessment was the general human inability to be objective. Viewed from a subjective perspective and choosing what I knew to be the right trait for the right situation, I looked like a reasonably good person most of the time. If ever there was a trait I wasn't fond of that matched my behavior, it was only in a certain scenario. I would rationalize, "I'm not angry all the time, so I wouldn't describe myself as an angry person."

We use all sorts of biases to justify unflattering behaviors. Left to our own devices, we may not have the most accurate read on who we are. So, although it was a self-assessment, I needed to solicit the opinions of people I interacted with to get an accurate account. For the best possible results, I questioned family members, close friends, coworkers, casual acquaintances, and a couple of people I spoke to once or twice in my entire life. If a pattern emerged and the data started to cluster, I could ascribe some validity to the feedback I received. Then I compared the data to my assessment to see if others' perceptions supported what I saw in the mirror or figure out how I could be so far off.

With the information collected, I knew what I needed to do to transform my actual self into my ideal self.

CHAPTER 5

THE CHOICE IS YOURS

CHOOSE YOUR TRAITS

Choice can be a blessing or a curse, depending on how we wield that power. Often, the power is misused or overlooked. Some of us engage in self-destructive behaviors, confrontations, and fixed mindsets that do not leave room for growth. Others fail to see opportunities to make changes that will produce more joy and personal satisfaction. How often have we heard the phrase "I don't have a choice"? That statement is rarely true.

We want the power of choice to work for us instead of against us, much like the mind itself. It is for that specific reason that we have the ability to choose. We are supposed to determine what will lead to a life that sees more joy than pain, more peace of mind, and less stress. We get to choose what we do with our lives (sometimes), who we want in our lives (most of the time), and most importantly, the type of person we want to be in our lives (all the time). Most of us forget this when life comes at us from every direction. We must never lose sight of our ability to decide who we want to be and how we want to act.

After taking the time to learn who I was, the time came to decide who I wanted to be. As I had discovered already, picking traits was complex. I knew I needed to do more than select traits that could vary from situation to situation. Instead of random positive traits, I selected what psychologist Gordon Allport described as cardinal traits to abide by. In this regard, I consider them more principles than traits, and I refer to them as the five pillars of self-centeredness. As I mentioned earlier, I chose to be a person who is humble, efficacious, accountable, resilient, and trustworthy.

After naming the characteristics I would like to exude, the question became "How do I do that?" I concluded there was a two-part answer to that question. Goal setting and—yes, Allen Iverson—practice!

◆ ◆ ◆

TRANSFORM YOUR TRAITS

When attempting to make a change or improve on a character trait, we must first clearly identify the characteristic we want to improve. For an example, let's choose patience as a goal because it is near and dear to my heart. I live with a person who struggles with being patient. I won't name names here, so we will call this person my wife to keep things anonymous.

Let's say my wife sends me a text message at noon: "Hey whatcha doin?"

If there is no response by 12:03, in comes a follow-up text. "Is your phone working? Did you get my message?"

Still no response from me. Another message at 12:05: "Are you ok? I'm starting to worry!"

The 12:07 message, number four, simply states, "Honey??????"

If I have not responded by 12:10, one of two scenarios will take place depending on her mood. Either she will file a report declaring me a missing person, or I am the worst husband and man in the entire world because whatever kept me away from my phone within the allotted time is far more important than her. In her mind, I no longer love her, she is not important, and I might as well take a long swim in the middle of the Pacific Ocean. In my case, that would be a creative way of telling me not to bother coming home ever again because I can't swim.

If you can relate to my wife as an impatient person or me as someone who lives with one, you likely see the need to practice being more patient. I like the SMART system for setting and achieving goals, but by all means, use whichever method works for you. Why do I like the SMART? Surprise! Because it's an acronym—for specific, measurable, attainable, relevant, and time based. Related to the example, my wife might aim to be more patient when interacting with people by text message.

She would start by sending a message to someone. Because her natural behavior is to hold her phone and stare at it until a reply appears, she might set a five-minute timer and place her phone face down until the timer goes off. If she accomplishes this, she has taken a step forward in improving her patience while executing all of the SMART elements. Her goal is measurable. Did she or did she not make it through the full five minutes without looking at her phone? It is also attainable. She is working in five-minute increments, so the feedback is quick. It is also relevant. This exercise is helping to improve her patience on a small scale, but successfully overcoming this challenge will lead to the ability to be patient for longer periods of time in different areas of her life. This goal is also time based; we can again refer to the five-minute timer. As the goal expands, so too will the time for achievement.

The goals must be measurable and attainable so adjustments can be made easily if necessary. If five minutes is too long, my wife can scale the timer back to three minutes or whatever amount of time seems attainable. After she experiences success, she can build on that to become more patient each time she engages in an exercise.

This technique can apply to any trait we believe needs improvement or should be introduced into our personality for the first time. In my case, I was aware of the five characteristics I would be focusing on, but I'd never made a concerted effort to live by those principles every day of my life.

Now that we have perspective, understanding, purpose, knowledge of who we are, the goal of who we want to be, and a method for becoming our ideal self, we are ready to add the HEART way of life to our personality and become self-centered.

CHAPTER 6

THE FIRST PILLAR—HUMILITY, THE PILLAR OF UNDERSTANDING

> Humility is the solid foundation of all virtues.
> —Confucius

The five principal pillars of the self-centered perspective embody all of the qualities a person needs for developing an introspective approach to life and to be fulfilled with that life despite harmful external stimuli. Many other qualities might be every bit as important as any that I list to be a well-balanced person, and I welcome you to determine your own foundation. The most important aspect of the principal pillars is to believe in them with all your heart (no pun intended). Our belief in what we are doing makes it easier to stay motivated to live by a code we can be proud of and that people will respect.

That said, the first pillar of the self-centered perspective is humility.

◆ ◆ ◆

WHAT IS HUMILITY?

The definition of humility is freedom from pride or arrogance. I wholeheartedly agree that we should abstain from arrogance, bragging, and the superiority complex that comes with affluence, whether of wealth or talent. I hesitate, however, to forgo pride altogether. Too much of any activity or action can lead to a poor outcome—

drinking too much alcohol, smoking too much weed, partying all the time, overeating, eating too much sugar or salt, sleeping too much, watching too much TV, etc. The list of overindulgences go on and on. Pride is the same way. Too much pride can be perceived as conceit, a trait people are not generally fond of. An overabundance of pride can also lie at the root of bad decisions and senseless suffering if we focus too much on avoiding uncomfortable feelings such as failure, embarrassment, and loneliness or showcasing how superior we are.

However, pride in the proper proportion is terrific for boosting self-esteem and provides a reason to put forth effort to achieve a goal. For example, we should take pride in the blessings and burdens of being human. When we think about all we can achieve with our unique ability to think and translate our thoughts into tangible accomplishments, inventions, innovations, art, technology, and architecture, it is impossible to argue that it's not a blessing to be born a human being.

Secondly, we should take pride in our DNA, which is loaded with pros and cons. Each of us has a unique genetic signature—even identical twins. Each of us is one of a kind, and that should be celebrated. We need to acknowledge who we are without prejudice or self-sabotage and recognize it is up to us to evolve into a self-centered person we can be proud of. Acknowledging our many flaws and faults is imperative because that inspires us to overcome those imperfections.

This acknowledgment is the basis for humility. A humble person understands that we are imperfect. We can take comfort in knowing it's not our fault if we are naturally angry, impatient, stingy, aloof, or any other character traits we would consider a challenge for those who have to interact with us. But we must take responsibility for areas where we fall short of our ideal self. Acknowledgment and acceptance of one's flaws are separate entities. Humility allows us to see our deficiencies as potential areas of development as opposed to a fixed label.

When we understand ourselves and the work it takes to experience personal growth, we can better empathize with other people lacking in certain areas of character development. We can better exude traits such as patience, supportiveness, and encouragement. Recognition of those flaws can make us more effective listeners and communicators when dealing with people. When we are humble, we demonstrate with our behavior that because we know we will never be a perfect finished product, we would never expect others to be perfect either. We can be objective and nonjudgmental. This perspective lays the groundwork for great interpersonal relationships. The way we conduct ourselves shines a light on what is possible in terms of positive human interaction if we choose to attempt to understand others by first gaining a solid understanding of ourselves.

◆ ◆ ◆

THE BALANCE OF PRIDE

It is essential not to let conceit burrow into our personality. Two scenarios can lead us to act and feel as if we are superior to other people: hard work and natural talent.

◆ HARD WORK

Scenario one is fruitful hard work. When we have put in the blood, sweat, and tears to reach an elite level of performance or a position of power within our chosen profession, we can become self-absorbed and broadcast a condescending aura in communicating with those we feel are inferior. If we earned our success, we might feel we have also earned the right to behave as an elitist. Of the two scenarios, the overindulgence of pride is more difficult to rein in here, especially if we have found success despite incredible odds stacked against us.

When we achieve our goals without the aid of blatant God-given talent or nepotism, we embody the great underdog story. In most cases, society loves to see a person with nothing but a dream, a strong belief in themselves, and tenacity that allows them to transform their dreams into reality (see David and Goliath). We should absolutely be proud of what we accomplish through our hard work, but instead of becoming arrogant, we would do better to focus on becoming an example for others to emulate.

Show and tell others what it took to get where you are, and encourage those who aspire to better themselves to use their unique qualities to accomplish their goals. Let them know you are a human being just like them and that if you were able to make good choices and execute the behaviors necessary for success, they can as well. Successful people who use their platform to lift others up are respected and revered for not only their talents but also their understanding of people and situations.

In my experience, powerful people who talk down to others or act superior tarnish their character and devalue the messages they attempt to communicate. Those treated as inferior, especially those with self-awareness, have no respect for that platform. This type of communication and interaction leads to toxic relationships and environments.

Beware of successes and accomplishments. They can have the same harmful effect as failure if humility is lost in the process of achievement.

♦ NATURAL TALENT

The second scenario involves understanding our God-given talents. As a society, we idolize people blessed with a genius brain, elite athletic ability, beautiful singing voice, rare physical attractiveness, or the ability to perform in a chosen profession at a high level with little effort. We call them special. We give them the title of "celebrity" and treat them as superior to other humans who lack their gifts.

I do not know how or why it became commonplace to revere superficial traits and abilities that do nothing to better our relationships with one another or make this world a safer place. I will preface my next comments by stating I have nothing against models or the modeling industry. I use this industry as an example of how humility can get lost amid external attention.

Models are typically chosen because they are outliers. They have a rare combination of facial beauty, seemingly flawless skin, slender or muscular frames, and above-average height. Yet as a society, we have accepted models as the beauty standard. The modeling industry chooses these unicorns as the spokespeople for fashion, fragrance, and jewelry, showcasing a beauty that most of us cannot relate to. The rest of us are left to believe that models' particular genetic makeup has more value than the average genetic sequence. Since most of us can never look like these people, we develop negative feelings such as jealousy, envy, and bitterness. Those feelings seep into our character, and we interact with the world from a resentful perspective. We develop complexes, low self-esteem, and insecurities about our appearance. In an attempt to emulate models, we might also develop eating disorders.

Because we treat naturally attractive models as transcendent beings, they sometimes act superior to us regular folk. The blessed, gifted, and successful can be demanding, arrogant, condescending, and dismissive because that feels natural to them.

The other side of that coin is the disrespect and unjust hate they receive because of their gifts. Those who resent celebrities' natural talents might make nasty comments out of jealousy and feel justified because these people are on television, and somehow that means they do not qualify as real people. We do not criticize their talent or blessings exclusively; in many cases, we criticize the human.

Crucially, humility helps us understand that we should never treat anyone as anything other than human. Those born with talent are still people at their core. Every celebrity or person of power has complex emotions to navigate just like the rest of us. If they go without food and water for too long, go without breathing for too long, or their heart stops beating, their life will expire just like that of any other human being. Mortality and vulnerability are the great equalizers.

Humility is a potent source of self-centeredness because it allows us to understand human nature by examining our own struggles and triumphs. It opens our eyes and inspires us to be more sympathetic, empathetic, and considerate when we see someone out of balance emotionally. We understand that each of us struggles with emotional competence. Humility also helps us be kind and supportive to those less fortunate genetically or environmentally. We understand that no one has a choice in their genetic foundation or the family they are born into. Making negative comments about a person's appearance or circumstances demonstrates an ignorance that a self-centered person will try to avoid. We are no more or less important than anyone else in the world from a human perspective.

Most importantly, with humility, we understand that no one is immune to hardship, especially psychologically. We may not share the same gifts as celebrities, but we do have gifts. Likewise, celebrities are saddled with imperfections just like everyone else.

We must never lose sight of the fact that we are humans before we are anything else. We should neither take nor give too much credit for unearned blessings. If you are one of the chosen few blessed with gifts the majority of people do not share, be grateful and understand you received those gifts by chance. Natural talent is something to be thankful for, not something to brag about. You did not sit down with God and create your human avatar. You did not choose the two people who made you.

Humility allows us to appreciate the foundation we were blessed with, minus the haughtiness that demeans what we accomplished with those gifts. Whether we are gifted or average, attractive or unattractive, successful or unsuccessful, if we give off the aura of being "down to earth" or "grounded," we are executing humility and, at least in part, living as a self-centered individual.

CHAPTER 7

THE SECOND PILLAR—EFFICACY, THE PILLAR OF BELIEVING

> People's beliefs about their abilities have a profound effect on those abilities.
> —Albert Bandura

WHAT IS EFFICACY?

I must preface the second pillar with a fundamental truth about our mindset regarding how we feel about ourselves, going back to humility. The fact that each of us is the only living organism with our specific genetic code makes us special, and we must recognize this to develop the second pillar of self-centeredness to where it needs to be.

The Beatles famously sang "All You Need is Love" back in 1967. I believe they were onto something, only they didn't quite finish the phrase. What they really meant was all you need is love for yourself. Loving ourselves lays the groundwork for believing in ourselves. We must love being the only one of us running around in the world. We must love that we are in charge of transforming our unique vessel into whatever we choose it to be. We are given the raw biological materials and should be grateful for the opportunity to make the most of it.

The old adage is true: "Whether you think you can or think you can't, you're right." I cannot emphasize enough how powerful our thoughts are and how they influence the way we conduct ourselves. The second pillar of efficacy, in short, means the power to produce an effect.

Since we are on a journey to attain self-centeredness, we want to focus on self-efficacy. Self-efficacy is a concept created by psychologist Alfred Bandura in 1977. The single most important factor leading to our successes and failures is what we believe about our life—what we believe we can achieve. That is why I refer to this pillar as the pillar of believing. It comprises our current self-assessment and our ideal self, wrapped in a single construct.

To mature, we must first have the desire to make changes and then the belief that we are capable of doing so. For those who enjoy a challenge, this will not be a difficult concept to master. Whether self-imposed or external, a challenge is a challenge, and those confident in their ability to compete will embrace the struggle to make personal changes and grow as a person. This is why efficacy is such an instrumental pillar for being self-centered. This mindset governs our self-worth and our motivation to succeed.

Unfortunately, we do not all possess the confidence necessary to accept who we are in the present or to believe change is possible. Which brings about a couple of questions: How do we develop our efficacy if it is low? What do we do if we do not have any efficacy at all?

The beauty of self-efficacy is there is more than one way to strengthen it.

◆ ◆ ◆

THE BEST TEACHER IS EXPERIENCE

The most effective way to grow self-efficacy is to draw confidence from past experiences. Our experiences give us tangible feedback that we can transform into competent behaviors. The first analogy that springs to mind is playing a video game that involves progressing through different levels.

The first time through a demanding part of the game can be a struggle. Our character dies immediately. The second time through, we die, but we do better than we did the first time. As this process continues, we become better at navigating the challenge until we eventually beat the level and move on to a more difficult one. We repeat that same process over and over until we eventually beat the game. If we went back and played the first level we initially struggled with, it would likely provide minimal challenge. The experience we gained taught us what to expect, and we devised a strategy to overcome the challenge. We experienced success before, so the belief in our ability to do it again is much stronger.

The greatest benefit of our personal experiences and the outcomes that transpire is they do not have to be positive to be useful. Learning what not to do can be just as beneficial as attempting to replicate a performance done correctly. Each situation we encounter that requires us to act grows our experience data bank. Notice in the video game analogy that many failures needed to occur. Every death served a purpose by teaching us a valuable lesson.

If we are attempting to control our emotions or learn a new skill, each success and failure can have a positive impact on our beliefs with the proper perspective. We learn which behaviors are effective and which are not, and we grow our self-efficacy by building on the behaviors that work and eliminating those that do not.

For those of us without the ability, resources, or circumstances to increase efficacy by way of personal achievement, we can find external assistance.

◆ ◆ ◆

VICARIOUS LIVING WITH A PURPOSE

The next best way to grow our efficacy is by watching others perform the behavior we are attempting to execute. In the case of growing our confidence, getting hands-on knowledge and insight into the thought process of confident people gives us a tangible reference point for where our mindset needs to be. Understanding how to think can significantly speed up the learning process.

Modern technology, especially related to the internet and YouTube-type platforms, has made vicarious learning a viable option for developing new behaviors. Between TED talks, motivational speakers, and content creators, it is almost impossible not to find someone who can help us with any given issue. In some cases, people lay out their exact blueprint for success, and ostensibly, all we have to do is follow their teachings and emulate their behaviors to accomplish our goals. Of course, we may find that the need to integrate someone else's personality into our own is a deal breaker, especially if they are an extrovert to our introvert. How can we develop our efficacy vicariously if we are the exact opposite of the person we are trying to learn from?

All hope is not lost in this situation. For one, the internet is vast. Chances are that someone out there has experienced similar success with a personality closer to our own. And if not, we might focus on the strategy as opposed to the personality of the prospective mentor and then find a unique way to implement the strategy to fit our personality and achieve the same success. It would be quite a confidence boost to be the first person to develop a guidebook to success for extreme introverts. Accomplish something like that, and self-efficacy goes through the roof!

◆ ◆ ◆

BE DOWN WITH OPP (OTHER PEOPLE'S PRAISE)

A third way to develop self-efficacy falls out of our control category. As we are all well aware, we do not get to choose our parents. These people shape the foundation of our development, whether positively or negatively. Theoretically, our parents should be our biggest supporters, teaching us valuable life lessons, instilling confidence, and boosting our self-esteem. Sadly, that is not always the case. For all types of reasons, parental influence may hinder our ability to develop healthy self-efficacy.

Again, all is not lost in this situation. If we did not have the encouraging home environment that taught us to believe in ourselves growing up, we can still luck our way into meeting people who will take an interest in us and our well-being. These people could be extended family members, teachers, counselors, and coaches who recognize our potential to be a good person and achieve success in our life endeavors. They pour their time and energy into guiding us because they believe in our capabilities, sometimes more than we do. Their external belief can spark an internal motivation that helps us start to believe in ourselves.

When people demonstrate they believe in us, we don't want to let them down, so we start behaving in the way they see us. Before long, the potential they saw is realized, and we become the highly functioning, successful person they insisted we could be. Sometimes someone telling us, "You can" is enough to inspire the determination to achieve our goals.

❖ ❖ ❖

THE IMPORTANCE OF EFFICACY

Believing in ourselves will always be in our best interest because there is no guarantee that anyone else will. If we do not believe in our capabilities, we can be quick to give up on ourselves and our dreams without even trying. Because the people around us often take cues from our energy, even the most positive people in our lives—those who try to be there for us and encourage us to be better—will lose hope.

If we don't strengthen our efficacy, we risk allowing others to determine what we are capable of. I don't know about you, but I take exception when people try to tell me what I can and cannot achieve. I take exception when another person attempts to break down my mental stability by labeling me a failure, lost cause, or loser if I happen to be going through a rough patch and haven't quite figured the way out. We must believe in ourselves because if we do not, it becomes easier to buy into the labels others bestow on us. We become a self-fulfilling prophecy.

Belief in ourselves leads to taking the action necessary to achieve our goals. Taking action leads to tangible experiences to bolster our self-efficacy. High self-efficacy is essential to the self-centered perspective. A self-centered person does not care when other people believe negative things about them. They are not disheartened by how many people before them failed to accomplish the same goals they have set for themselves. Attacking life from the self-centered perspective gives us the motivation and discipline required to achieve whatever goals we believe lie within our capability.

CHAPTER 8

THE THIRD PILLAR—ACCOUNTABILITY, THE PILLAR OF INTROSPECTION

> I believe that accountability is the basis of all meaningful human achievement.
> —Sam Silverstein

WHAT IS ACCOUNTABILITY?

We are all probably familiar with the phrase "Nobody likes a tattletale." Our third pillar, in part, is a testament to that notion because the focus is on ourselves instead of pointing the finger at others. The third pillar in the foundation of self-centeredness is accountability.

A suitable definition of what it means to be accountable is the willingness to accept responsibility for one's actions. When someone takes responsibility, it's easier to determine the next steps. Whether it be punishment or forgiveness, we can deal with the issue and move on. I am confident we have all encountered people who seem acutely allergic to accepting responsibility when situations do not go according to plan. These situations are especially frustrating when we can identify the responsible party.

In our quest to become self-centered, we need to go deeper than a textbook definition of accountability, not only because it sits right in the middle of the HEART acronym but also because it perfectly illustrates what self-centeredness is all about. Accountability is the pillar of introspection. We take a fully introspective view of a situation foremost, in all situations, all the time.

There are two forms of accountability we must master to become self-centered: situational accountability and personal accountability. Taking responsibility for our part in a situation and focusing on how to improve our own actions provides us the opportunity to demonstrate effective leadership while keeping ourselves emotionally balanced.

◆ ◆ ◆

SITUATIONAL ACCOUNTABILITY

The ability to focus exclusively on one's own role in a situation involving more than one person is what I refer to as situational accountability. This type of accountability is relevant in scenarios such as collaborative work or school efforts, phone conversations with customer service, driving on the road with other motorists, or any circumstance involving human interaction. In these situations, we should focus only on our own actions for three important reasons: it curbs expectations we set for other people, it strengthens our character, and it is good for our mental and physical health.

Interpersonal relations and the issues they create crop up every day. We sometimes work with unreliable people or people we don't have a good rapport with. We may need to see a doctor when we experience something unusual concerning our health. We might put our kids in sports to help them learn the values of hard work, preparation, teamwork, and sportsmanship. The mistake we often make lies in the expectations we set for other people.

Humility has taught us people are not infallible. We should not expect people to behave or perform as we believe they should. I understand the logic behind expecting each group member to execute their assigned task. I understand the logic behind expecting a doctor to be competent with diagnosis and treatment. I understand the logic behind expecting our kids to improve as people and players under the guidance of a coach. The problem is that despite titles and responsibilities, we are all only human. When we set expectations and they inevitably go unfulfilled, we often suffer the consequences more than the person who has let us down. By consequences I mean we put ourselves in a position to deal with our own negative emotions and potential negative behavior.

For example, think about the dining experiences you've had in restaurants and whether the service by the waiter or waitress was not very good, average, or exceptional. When I considered this scenario, I realized how rare it is for a waiter or waitress to be outstanding. It is far more common for me to have an average or below-average experience at a restaurant, so where does that expectation for excellent service come from? Somehow, the few restaurants with great service become the expected standard for every waiter or waitress to live up to. However, having that expectation sets me up for disappointment every time the standard isn't met.

When our expectations aren't fulfilled, we tend to be more judgmental and make comparisons where they aren't warranted. People and situations should be evaluated on a case-by-case basis. By not setting expectations, we can navigate our experiences objectively and avoid having negative feelings to process in a situation; we understand mistakes, incompetency, and bad days are part of the human condition and that the people we interact with could be experiencing one of those issues when our paths cross. This prevents us from being rude or exorbitantly decreasing the amount we might leave for a tip. Understanding that we humans are not at our best every day and empathizing with that notion is one way our character remains high quality.

If we are not mindful of our emotions, our character can suffer a setback when people fall short of expectations. I mentioned being judgmental when this occurs, but anger and frustration are also common emotions when people let us down. In those emotional states, we are more apt to yell, demean, or demonstrate aggressive behavior to express our disappointment. These are the types of behaviors we want to avoid. Instead of allowing our emotions to dictate how we behave, situational accountability suggests we look at the actions we can take to improve a situation or find a solution to a problem. Instead of blaming someone for their inability to help us or getting upset by it, we figure out another way to get the help we need.

Here we return to the issue of what we control and what we do not. Doesn't it feel better not to rely on someone else, especially if that person is someone we don't know personally? At the very least, if we take the matter into our own hands, we know a genuine effort is being made on our behalf to get the solution we are seeking. We must not waste time disparaging others for their shortcomings. If the person we are dealing with offers little to no assistance, the best response is to move on to the next possible solution. Keeping our emotions in check and not pointing fingers will earn respect from those around us. This perspective not only attests to our character but can also benefit us mentally and physically.

I am sure we are familiar with phrases that express how angry we can get. For instance, "My blood was boiling" or "I just saw red." Situational accountability helps us when we feel this way because it forces us to focus on our feelings instead of the person or event that triggered them. We are cognizant of our anger as well as the harmful effects of that particular emotion.

We have already discussed how being angry can alter our behavior and lead us to those infamous "out of character" moments we often regret. If not managed correctly in real time, anger can do more than hurt our reputation. Angry people typically experience higher levels of stress and anxiety, which can lead to physical health issues that decrease quality of life, such as poor sleeping habits, high blood pressure, strokes, and heart failure; they may also lead to a mood disorder, such as depression, or to addiction to cope with negative feelings. Situational accountability reminds us we have a responsibility to ourselves to behave in a manner beneficial to our own mental and physical health. We keep our mind off the upsetting event and focus solely on how we should respond in accordance with our personal accountability.

❖ ❖ ❖

PERSONAL ACCOUNTABILITY

Personal accountability is probably the most critical aspect of the self-centered perspective. It is how we keep ourselves in balance. The leading expert on what events bring us joy and misery and the type of person we wish to be is us, and only us. Staying true to ourselves and not allowing external influence to influence our character is how we remain centered in a world attempting to pull us in many different directions.

Allowing outside sources that do not have our best interest in mind to influence us is far too common. I do not understand why fitting in with the masses is so important. I have heard stories of people sacrificing happiness and compromising their morals to fulfill a psychological need to belong. Everyone wants to be considered "normal," even though normal is a subjective concept. It is imperative that we decide for ourselves who we are and how we conduct ourselves out in the world. Once we make that decision, we must be proud of it. We mustn't allow ourselves to be guilted or shamed into acting like someone we are not. It is more than okay to go against the grain, especially when holding ourselves accountable to the standards we set for ourselves.

The most taxing aspect of personal accountability is blocking out external influences that kindle negative emotions within us. Whenever we are mistreated, disrespected, or taken advantage of, we tend to focus on the negative event and how that influence made us feel. These situations are the ultimate test of our commitment. If we want to become self-centered, we cannot allow outside influence, especially another person, to dictate how we handle ourselves.

So often I hear people say they feel as though they need to match the energy they receive. A quote often attributed to my man Gandhi states, "An eye for an eye will leave the whole world blind." This observation sheds light on the fact that when we match our energy with someone else's negative energy, nobody wins. Matching wits with someone's ignorance gives the illusion we are sticking up for ourselves because our emotions are involved. We satisfy a primal urge to defend ourselves. The simple reality, however, is we are now just as ignorant as the person we are dealing with. Matching ignorance with ignorance leaves the whole world dumb.

As self-centered people, we seek balance, so we must counter negative energy with positive energy, ignorance with intelligence, the irrational with the rational. We do this by holding ourselves personally accountable to the principles by which we live. We stand by these principles at all times, under any circumstance, never allowing our emotions to get off center.

CHAPTER 9

THE FOURTH PILLAR—RESILIENCE, THE PILLAR OF EFFORT, WILL, AND ACTION

> In order to succeed, people need a sense of self-efficacy, to struggle together with resilience to meet the inevitable obstacles and inequities of life.
>
> —**Albert Bandura**

Real change cannot take place without putting in the work. Improving any skill takes practice and repetition. When it comes to strengthening the core of our personality, the labor required can feel daunting. We need a powerful sense of purpose to keep us going, and there is no greater purpose than self-improvement. The drive to keep pushing leads us to the fourth pillar, which is resilience.

◆ ◆ ◆

WHAT IS RESILIENCE?

Resilience is defined as the ability to recover from or adjust easily to misfortune or change. That is a great definition covering, in part, what we need to do to achieve our goals. When it comes to being self-centered, however, we must once again go a little deeper.

If you are old enough to read this book, chances are you have experienced adversity. Big or small, I guarantee that at some point, challenges have impeded your ability to be happy or maintain a positive mindset all the time. Resilience is a valuable trait because it battles with our most dangerous adversary: our emotions. We are gifted and cursed with the ability to experience complex emotions. When aspects of our life are going well, we can feel elated to the point of euphoria, and nothing can get us down. On the other hand, when life gives us nothing but hardships, challenges, and pain, we feel defeated, sad, and empty. Bad experiences have a far greater impact on our psyche than good ones. To add insult to injury, our emotions are instinctive, so we cannot control them, and our knee-jerk response is often unflattering behavior. This tendency is a natural phenomenon we have all encountered.

This penchant for dwelling on the negative is our greatest obstacle to overcome. We are constantly getting hammered over the head by negative people, uncontrollable tragedies, childhood trauma, and countless negative thoughts that make us our own worst enemy. Believe me, there is enough external negativity to block the path to our goals for an entire lifetime. We do not need our mind working against us as well! Facing opposition and suffering major setbacks when striving for a goal is inevitable. Understanding that humans are hardwired to focus more on the bad in life, we must make the extra effort to be mindful of the good things. We must remember we still have a choice in our actions.

Being resilient allows us to keep our eyes on the prize and persevere through the challenging times. Increasing resilience will boost our work ethic as well. We will work harder and smarter, no matter the obstacle, because we understand that the job has to get done despite what stands in the way.

◆ ◆ ◆

MENTAL TOUGHNESS

To be resilient also means to have a strong will. With our self-efficacy securely in place, a strong will gives us an advantage over others aspiring to the same goal who do not possess that attribute. Resilience gives us the comfort of knowing it is impossible for someone to outwork us. No matter how many times we are told no, we will not relent until we get a yes. No matter how often we fail at a task, we will continue to learn and grow from those mistakes until success is achieved.

When we are resilient, we understand that running on a treadmill of negative self-talk, self-pity, and excuses to justify giving up won't get us any closer to reaching our goals. Time is a luxury that once wasted is unrecoverable. The scariest realization we must face is there is no time like the present to keep our life moving forward on the path to self-centeredness. When we have ambition, choosing to remain in the same place is almost the same as going backward. A resilient person never gives up and never accepts stagnation. Most importantly, a resilient individual never dwells on the negative.

Resilience in the framework of being self-centered focuses on taking action in the face of adversity. The most essential element to solving a problem is the actual solving of the problem. Resilient people keep their focus on what will have a positive impact on the bottom line.

CHAPTER 10

THE FIFTH PILLAR—TRUST, THE ULTIMATE PILLAR

As soon as you trust yourself, you will know how to live.

—Johann Wolfgang von Goethe

Being a trustworthy individual is vital. Try applying for a home loan or a high line of credit as a person known for being untrustworthy. A lack of trust from financial institutions will lead to many rejections, astronomical interest rates, and cosigners.

Think about how safe the world would be if we could all trust one another. We could let our kids play outside or walk home from school, and we could skip the panic attack that comes with feeling like they aren't safe. How nice would it be to leave our house and not lock the door? To go to work and not lock the car? Kids would have no need for locks on their school lockers. We could be certain our children wouldn't be bullied or picked on for any reason. Can you imagine being in the comfort of your home, work, school, or out on the town for date night, feeling 100 percent safe from any kind of harm because every person on this earth can be trusted? The stress and anxiety I feel leaving my body just thinking about it is incredible.

As an aside, to be totally transparent here, this thought brought on a feeling of security that I do not normally have. For a moment, as I wrote, the sentiment of heaven on earth felt attainable. I paused my writing to daydream about a trustworthy world in a blissful and serene state of being. It was nice. And then a voice filled the air: "Honey, don't forget to pick up our daughter from practice right at four o'clock. I don't like her waiting out there all alone"—my wife, snapping me back to the reality we live in where people actually scheme to abduct little girls.

All that said, the fifth and final pillar of the self-centered perspective is trust.

◆ ◆ ◆

WHAT IS TRUST?

Trust is an interesting pillar. Not only does it represent ethics, which guide our understanding of right and wrong, but it also summarizes the other four pillars. The simplest definition of trust is to be dependable or worthy of confidence. In the self-centered spectrum, to be trustworthy means being honest with ourselves and making every effort to engage in the right course of action.

It is a bit of an old-school perspective, but I believe our word should be equal to any legally binding contract. We must say what we mean, mean what we say, and follow through with action. If we engage in this pattern of behavior consistently enough, we can earn the trust of those around us.

As we have already discussed, trust has incredibly high value, all the more so because it is extremely fragile. Going back to humans homing in on life's negatives, when trust is broken between people, it is almost impossible to restore. When entering any relationship where trust is a big factor in determining the fruitfulness of the union, earning and keeping that trust is crucial.

◆ ◆ ◆

TRUST AND THE OTHER PILLARS

Each of the other four pillars can help in earning, keeping, and increasing trust. If we show *humility,* we can be relatable, and when people can relate to us, trust develops. If our *efficacy* is high, we are steady in our beliefs. People appreciate consistency; those who waver in their convictions are far less trustworthy than those who stand by their word and principles regardless of circumstance. *Accountability* is almost synonymous with being trustworthy. When people know we will take responsibility for our words and actions, they will trust us. Our *resilience* shows people they can rely on us to do whatever it takes to live up to our word.

◆ ◆ ◆

THE PERSON IN THE MIRROR

As important as trust is to building relationships, being honest with ourselves is most important. This ability kick-starts the whole self-assessment where we compare our actual self to our ideal self. Being honest with ourselves is the only way to experience real growth. We do not have to feel shame or inadequacy for our shortcomings because the assessment is between us and the mirror only. If we know we are telling ourselves the truth about who we are, the self-assessment does not need to go further than that. The plan for personal growth can start taking shape without delay. But if we are not honest with ourselves, very little growth is possible.

Convincing ourselves we don't need to work on anything will only perpetuate a cycle of negative experiences, emotions, and outcomes. This is a dangerous precedent. By now, we should realize that other people cannot always be trusted; if we are also lying to ourselves, we might have no one looking out for our best interests. We at least need the comfort of knowing the person in the mirror always has our back. We have to be real with ourselves. It is much easier to navigate life as a trustworthy individual who trusts him or herself.

CHAPTER 11

NAVIGATING DIFFICULT INTERNAL LIFE EXPERIENCES

We have discussed the unpredictable nature of life and the psychological roller coasters we ride thanks to our emotional responses. Dealing with negative events in real time is imperative. Minimizing or eliminating the harmful effects of chronic or festering negative feelings and behaviors benefits our mental health, physical well-being, and overall quality of life. Each of our lives teem with unique challenges to overcome. Although many challenges vary, there are also quite a few more universal ones. We will discuss some common life events we all deal with in our quest to remain self-centered and live a balanced life.

◆ ◆ ◆

NAVIGATING NEGATIVITY

> I will not let anyone walk through my mind with their dirty feet.
> —Attributed to Mahatma Gandhi

Our life is frequently invaded by adverse events both controllable and uncontrollable. One common denominator lies at the root of almost every negative situation. Can you guess what that is? Or more to the point, *who* it is? It's people! With the exception of natural disasters, the vast majority of events that make life more difficult involve interactions with other people. We too are people, so of course we can be our own worst enemy at times.

With people, negativity can rear its ugly head in the most critical areas of our life. It can also be found in fleeting encounters with strangers, either in person, on the phone, or on social media. Negativity is like an infectious airborne plague. Remain in its presence for too long, and it can contaminate the mind, darken our mood, and negatively influence our behavior. Whatever scenario we are facing, it is important to remember humility. When we encounter a person who never has anything productive to contribute to a conversation or situation, we should take the time to examine why that is. More than likely, the person who never seems happy, is always complaining, and never wants others to do well developed that mindset through their life experiences.

I believe negative people and negativity itself stem from emotions like stress, anger, anxiety, jealousy, and depression, to name a few. When people experience these in high volume, these negative emotions become part of their daily disposition, which influences their behavior. Negativity attracts and feeds off more negativity. As the saying goes, "Misery loves company." Negative people seem content only when everyone else is as miserable as they are.

As self-centered people, we must not be influenced or affected by another person's negativity. The root cause of their behavior comes from their life experiences, so it is essential not to allow their inner turmoil to become our own. We counter negativity with positivity to keep negative energy from growing and making situations worse. If we stay true to our principles, negativity will not find a suitable host through which to grow and spread.

When negative people attempt to infiltrate our mind with counterproductive commentary, insults, and prognostications, the key to minimizing the effect is an accountability mindset involving a healthy perspective—namely, an understanding of what we do and do not control. We know we cannot control someone else's negative perspective. We do, however, control our response to their negativity, and life is too unpredictable to waste time not enjoying every second we get.

I mentioned humility as instrumental in handling these situations because it allows us to understand the opposing point of view. Meanwhile, accountability protects us from adopting negativity into our disposition because we focus on ourselves instead of the negative stimuli. When faced with these encounters, we reflect on the situation internally and focus on what we could have done to bring about a more positive outcome. Taking this approach eliminates the need to exclusively blame others or harbor ill will toward someone with a negative disposition. Moving on from a negative situation does not require the other party to admit fault or take the blame. If our assessment sees someone else's actions as the direct cause of a negative outcome, there is no need to point the finger at that person.

Even in cases where we face unjust blame, we simply state the facts that prove we are not to blame rather than openly throwing others under the bus. There is a code on the streets: "Snitches get stitches." This is to say, when we point the finger at someone else, we may be physically assaulted. I don't know about you, but I prefer my skin unsewn! There is also an unwritten rule that there is honor in not snitching or being a tattletale.

Of course, there are exceptions. For severe offenses against humanity where people are being hurt, taken against their will, or wrongfully accused of a serious offense, the code goes out the window because we would all benefit from a society that sees no violence, no unjust punishments, and no evil intent toward our fellow humans.

As crazy as it may seem not to point the finger at those who are responsible for a transgression, we gain respect as people who can be trusted by everyone involved in the situation. If we are respected and trusted, we can be leaders. As leaders, we can influence people with our behavior alone; those who respect us will follow our example. When a situation requires someone to own up to a mistake, the people around us will step up and be accountable because they know that's what we would do, and they appreciate that quality.

Hopefully, as humans we can evolve to a place where we do not need to blame others for negative encounters in order to feel good about ourselves. In the meantime, when dealing with negative people, we must be humble enough to consider their point of view but accountable enough to the mirror and the principles by which that reflection lives to remain uninfluenced mentally and behaviorally by someone else's negativity.

♦ ♦ ♦

NAVIGATING EMOTIONS

> "Emotion can be the enemy. If you give into your emotion, you lose yourself. You must be at one with your emotions, because the body always follows the mind."
>
> **—Attributed to Bruce Lee**

In my humble opinion, the most challenging part of being human is learning how to navigate emotion. We are genetically predisposed to respond to life experiences in the manner our unique DNA dictates. Since emotions are naturally occurring physiological responses to certain stimuli, our behavioral responses also feel natural. The best chance we have to process our emotions in a healthy way is to be armed with three key areas of understanding: which elements of life we control and which we do not, our biological makeup, and the power of choice in manifesting health and well-being.

The first realization we need to accept is we cannot control our emotions. If people around us suggest we be more emotional or less emotional in our communication or behavior, we are being asked to do the impossible. If you happen to be a hypersensitive person, please do not let other people convince you that you have a problem. If you happen to be on the opposite end of the emotional spectrum and people describe you as emotionally unavailable, robotic, or dead inside, there is absolutely nothing wrong with that either. Nobody is qualified to tell us what our normal is because normal is a subjective concept.

For an example, we might look at two 16-month-old babies placed in a room full of toys. They are allowed to play with whichever toy they choose. Once they select a toy, a parent or authority figure might come in and take the toy away from the child. Let's suppose the same scenario for both children, but child number one throws a full-blown tantrum. Tears are flowing, skin tone is a lovely reddish purple, and self-inflicted cranium bashing on the floor is taking place. It is an absolute catastrophe for that child to have lost that toy. In contrast, when the toy is taken away from child number two, there is no crying. In fact, there is barely any reaction. Child number two simply picks a different toy to play with.

In this scenario, it would be natural to assume child number two has their act together and that this is how a child should behave. That perspective is okay if we are stating a preference because a preference is simply a desire or a wish. But what we wish for and reality often do not coincide. A real-life healthy perspective would acknowledge and accept where our child's temperament is at this early stage and devise a plan to teach them to process their emotions healthily as they get older. With age comes experiences that can significantly alter perspective.

If we are the parent of child number two, we should hold off on patting ourselves on the back. At sixteen months old, that child is much too young to understand complex emotions. Future life events between sixteen months and sixteen years could completely reshape how that child processes a negative interaction. They may grow up and become extremely angry at a perceived injustice based on experiences that profoundly impacted their psyche. Our well-behaved sixteen-month-old is simply responding in their natural way. In this case, it is our job as a parent to recognize this trait and nurture, cultivate, and strengthen that behavior so they grow up with the ability to keep situations in perspective and make rational decisions. If we do that successfully, now we can pat ourselves on the back and take a bow because we have done well!

If we are the parent of child number one, the same principles apply. The temper tantrum behavior is not a fixed one. As a parent, we have to recognize when our child appears to be hypersensitive to specific life experiences; more than likely, they will have a strong emotional response to the different stimuli life has to offer. They must be educated on their emotions and taught how to manage them effectively, just like child number two. If child number one has a tantrum every time a toy is taken, that is normal behavior for that child. If child number two never has a tantrum when a toy is taken away, that is normal behavior for that child. Two completely different responses can be considered normal within the context of each child's DNA.

The critical aspect of this scenario is how similar scenarios are handled going forward. Whether we need to reinforce or redirect, handling life circumstances is how our emotional intelligence takes shape. Emotions cannot be stopped or even controlled, and we should not attempt to do so. Instead, we need to acknowledge how a situation makes us feel and take a pause.

Few of us can do this automatically because it feels so natural to react in the heat of the moment with our physiological response leading the way. Our goal to become a well-balanced, self-centered person with emotional intelligence hinges on the ability to take that pause. It makes all the difference in a situation becoming agreeable or disagreeable.

Our varying genetics and life experiences determine the emotions we have to navigate around or through, but some are more common than others. I will look at a few emotions, feelings, and circumstances we are all likely to encounter and offer my perspective on them in hopes of providing an alternative way to look at different situations—a way that will help us live with less negativity, less conflict, more peace, more joy, and manageable stress.

◆ ◆ ◆

NAVIGATING STRESS

> The greatest weapon against stress is our ability
> to choose one thought over another.
> **—Attributed to William James**

Most of us are sure to encounter stress in some form or another. Stress is basically the physical and psychological strain we feel when confronted with external situations that are uncomfortable or have deadlines. If we looked for it, we could find stress in almost every situation. Stress in its different forms and situations could fill the pages of an entire book all by itself. For our purposes, we will discuss a few of the most common types of stress and stressful situations, along with suggestions on how to combat those situations productively.

Since we are all on a path to achieving self-centeredness, it is important to view stress from a self-preservation perspective. We will lean on our self-centered pillars to help guide our actions. In the case of stress, the three primary pillars are efficacy, accountability, and resilience.

First, we need to acknowledge that our stress persists due to our negative thoughts. That is where accountability works to our benefit. Once we recognize that we largely create our own stress, it becomes easier to believe that stress is manageable and, most importantly, that if we are the cause of our prolonged stress, we are also the solution. This is where our efficacy comes into play. Believing in our ability to put stress in the proper perspective to manage it effectively is a critical aspect of being self-centered.

Resilience is activated by recognizing the types of life events that cause us stress as individuals and understanding that all stressful situations have a solution to strive for. Whatever the stressor, we must act despite how we feel, or the stress might consume us. We either engage in behaviors that help prevent the situations from happening, or we find solutions for problems that could not be avoided in the moment. The singular purpose of engaging in behaviors to reach a solution helps us navigate and cope with stress without thinking about the actual stressor.

There are many distinct types of stress. I will focus on a few of them now.

♦ ACUTE STRESS

One common type of stress is surprise or acute stress. This stress springs on us without warning, such as when we show up for work on the day of a big meeting that could land the company a multimillion-dollar account and the boss says, "By the way, the guy that's been in charge of this project from the beginning, Mark, is out sick today. The meeting cannot be rescheduled. This is our only opportunity to make this happen, so you will have to take his place. Everybody is gathered in the conference room. You have five minutes to get organized. Don't forget, this account alone will make or break the stability of our company, and many of our jobs are on the line. Good luck!" This is the job equivalent of walking into class unprepared for a dreaded pop quiz that is worth so many points it will hurt our grade if we don't do well.

Spontaneous stress is tough due to the nature of its occurrence. Because it pops up without warning, we can't deal with it logically or process options thoroughly. Sudden onset stress is best dealt with ahead of time, by building resilience. A resilient person understands preparedness is one of the best techniques to combat the unexpected. In the case of the meeting, the best strategy should have already taken place before receiving that news.

A sports analogy explains how stress might be eliminated in this situation. In football, injuries are a common occurrence, so there is always a backup plan to account for the loss of a player. If the starting quarterback gets injured, the backup quarterback has to take his place. A common strategy for the backup quarterback is to practice as though he were the starter. That way, if the starting quarterback sustains an injury, the backup quarterback is equally prepared to come in and lead the team.

In the office example, if we prepare to lead the meeting in the first place, even if the scenario seems unlikely, we are ready for an acutely stressful situation such as Mark coming down with an illness. We would be less stressed about stepping into the leadership role because we are ready for the opportunity. This applies to anyone with the ambition of ascending the ranks in a business hierarchy. If we perform our job to the best of our abilities while also preparing for the job we aspire to, we set ourselves up for success.

We never know when an opportunity or a stressful situation might present itself, so it is in our best interest to live the Boy Scout motto and be prepared. In either scenario, being prepared will give us confidence to handle the situation because we don't have to pause to think about our actions. We already know what to do, so we avoid negative feelings such as panic and anxiety, thereby keeping our mental health in balance.

♦ CHRONIC STRESS

On the opposite end of surprise or acute stress is chronic stress. This type of stress is brought on by certain family members, our jobs, living with an illness or handicap, taking care of a loved one who is ill or disabled, parenting, money, the commute to work, or any circumstance that causes ongoing daily stress. This type of stress is the most harmful because the symptoms can hinder our mental and physical health.

Living in a constant state of worry negatively affects our behavior and relationships if we allow the stress to compound day after day. Eventually the metaphorical weight will crush our spirit, leading to a life devoid of passion, excitement, and joy, replaced with hopelessness, sadness, and a melancholy state of mind. If we do not deal with our chronic stress, we run the risk of developing serious health concerns, such as heart attack, stroke, and depression.

Chronic stress often manifests in unavoidable circumstances, but unavoidable does not mean those circumstances cannot be dealt with in a healthy manner. When it comes to dealing with people, the first method requires effective communication. This means conversing with the person causing the stress to understand their perspective, establishing clear parameters, setting boundaries, or whatever is necessary for the interaction to be less stressful.

This conversation should be measured, calm, and calculated rather than devolving into finger-pointing. We must avoid assessing blame and starting every sentence with "You need to . . ." This comes off as combative and accusatory, and our message will be lost amid the other person's defensiveness as they respond to a perceived attack. They will not acknowledge our words, just our approach. Instead of solving a problem, we now have an additional one because a perceived combative approach typically leads to disagreements.

We must instead use an introspective approach and focus on ourselves. We can let the person know how we are feeling and what we think we can do to improve the interaction, then ask how they are feeling and how they think we can resolve the interaction between us through a collaborative effort. This nonconfrontational way to find a solution for our stress is more likely to produce a favorable outcome. By showing accountability, we keep them away from a defensive mindset and foster an open mind where they are willing to listen to what we say and make an effort to work with us on the issue.

Inanimate chronic stressors such as finances or traffic must first be approached by controlling the controllable elements in the situation. I don't want to go into detail on this because the controllable elements will vary from person to person, but there is probably an action we can take to ease our stress. The other countermeasure for chronic stress is adding or increasing daily activities that bring us joy for balance: activities such as reading, journaling, watching television, exercising, or meditating, to name a few. The self-centered perspective always seeks balance for our state of mind.

I have a relatable story from my personal life when it comes to dealing with chronic stress. My wife is one of the most selfless people on the planet. Selflessness may sound like a great trait, but it can also make her one of the most miserable people on the planet. One school of thought suggests we treat other people better than we treat ourselves. Unfortunately, my wife takes that to heart, and that is how she lives her life. She is incredibly giving and caring. It's great for her employer, my kids, and myself because she takes care of us on a superhuman level. However, giving only to others and never to ourselves becomes exhausting.

I see it in her facial expressions, I hear it in her voice, and it breaks my heart every time I can tell she has reached her limit. The problem is, it's not just us and all of our issues paired with a job that stresses her out. Her commute is stressful. She is a clean freak, so a few dishes in the sink is stressful. She is a people pleaser, so living each day trying to live up to the expectations of others while not making mistakes is a very stressful way of life. She accumulates unnatural amounts of stress with no outlet for it. When the stress overwhelms her, an inevitable breakdown follows, featuring either an angry explosion where we all run for cover or a deep sadness. Neither of those responses is beneficial for anyone. Especially her.

Because I love her and I hate to see her go through that, I try to give exclusively to her in the way she gives to the family. I want her to know we appreciate her and we care for her mental well-being. The problem with this solution is I am merely human. I fail at times to acknowledge her efforts, support her when she is struggling mentally, or comfort her at the exact time she needs it. That is why we have to take time for ourselves. Only we know when we need a positive experience to balance the negative.

When I suggest this to my wife, her classic comeback is always "What time?" Meaning, "I don't have time to take for myself." That mindset is the flaw of being selfless and treating others better than yourself. I wholeheartedly disagree with that sentiment. Other people do not have more value than us, so why treat them like they do? Other people's time is not more precious than ours, so why give all of it away?

If we're out there constantly doing for others while neglecting our mental health, we are doing ourselves a disservice. Even the Bible states that the good deeds we do on earth will not punch our ticket to H-Town. There is also no rule stating that we must put ourselves through hell on earth to walk through the pearly gates. So, in my opinion, that level of self-sacrifice is unwarranted and unhealthy behavior. If we feel we don't have time for ourselves, we need to make time. We don't want to rely on other people to show their appreciation or gratitude for all our sacrifices because there is no guarantee we will receive it. Even if we receive it, there is no guarantee it will come in the manner we would like.

We must take the time to engage in whatever activity it takes to lose ourselves in joy to balance out all that stress and negativity. We can avoid emotional meltdowns altogether, and our minds will thank us by being clear and focused on a healthier perspective.

◆ EVENT-BASED STRESS

Another type of stress is what I refer to as event-based stress. Some specific events that cause stress include public speaking, performing, meeting new people, or driving at night. This stress reveals itself when we realize we will have to engage in one of these uncomfortable situations in the near future. If we don't manage this dangerous stress properly, it could lead to anxiety. If anxiety gets too high, we can suffer full-blown panic attacks.

Event-based stress can be dealt with effectively by practicing the events that stress us out. There is a positive correlation between increased competency and comfort. The greater our competency in performing a task, the greater our comfort level will be and, subsequently, the less stress we will experience in those situations.

◆ EMOTIONAL STRESS

The last type of stress on my short list is stress triggered by our emotions. This stress might occur due to thoughts of a traumatic experience, thoughts of uncertainty, an abusive relationship, toxic relationships at work, or with acquaintances. No matter what we are thinking about, we can deal with it in a healthy way. We can put our stressors in the proper perspective and live to the best of our ability.

Traumatic stress can be a major psychological roadblock for people. First and foremost, I would recommend seeking a licensed professional therapist to assist with effective coping strategies to help work through those complex thoughts and feelings. There is no shame in therapy, just as there is no shame in asking for help. I happen to believe therapy is beneficial for everyone. That said, when I share my thoughts, I do so not as a licensed professional but rather as a human being sharing my perspective on life.

As I mentioned earlier, to effectively combat stress, we must understand that we perpetuate that stress with our thoughts. It is up to us to stop our brain from focusing on the wrong issue. If we remain in automatic mode, our emotions dictate how we feel and act; our emotions are much too unstable for that kind of responsibility. When we get caught up in this cycle, we must switch the shifter in our mind from automatic to manual so we can decide for ourselves how to process the way we are feeling and formulate a strategy to cope effectively.

The stressor is the known factor, so we can move on from that thought. Dwelling on traumatic stress is counterproductive and will only worsen the way we feel. Instead of focusing on the bad hand we were dealt, the person or people making our lives more difficult, or the feeling we get when an uncomfortable situation is looming, we must turn our attention to what we control. We control the actions we take to fix a situation, reverse a situation, prevent a situation from getting worse, or prevent a stressful situation from happening at all. As I stated earlier, our efficacy, accountability, and resilience will guide us. The most critical element in a stressful situation is us.

We are in control of our stress. We must not allow a stressful situation to dictate how we feel or behave. Belief in our power to choose how we respond is how we become self-centered.

◆ ◆ ◆

NAVIGATING LONELINESS

> Pray that your loneliness may spur you into finding something to live for, great enough to die for.
>
> —Dag Hammarskjold

For a long time, the term "lonely" was defined as a state of solitude or being isolated from human contact. This physical form of loneliness is easy to remedy. We can visit bars, nightclubs, malls, grocery stores, gyms, and many other public places to surround ourselves with people. It is slightly more complicated if our loneliness is romantic in nature; the lack of a companion to share our lives with seems to heighten the feeling.

The best way to conquer this brand of loneliness is to pour all our available energy into growing ourselves as a person. We can read and learn. Becoming a master of the five pillars of self-centeredness boosts the power of the mind and allows us to be at peace with who we are at all times. We can exercise consistently and eat a healthy diet to improve our physical health and become hyper-focused on taking care of ourselves in every way. These activities can boost confidence, and when we project confidence, we increase the likelihood of meeting the right person to fill that void in our life.

To be alone is not the only type of loneliness. The definition has now evolved into a complicated mindset where physically being alone is sometimes not even a factor. This state of mind is more about a feeling than the physical environment around us. Anytime we deal with the way we feel, we must lean on our efficacy. Our efficacy arms us with the belief that we can choose how to handle the way we feel and control the duration of any feeling. Emotions are out of our control by nature, so preventing the feeling in the moment is impossible. But like many life circumstances, understanding the why is critical in finding an effective solution.

We have to figure out for ourselves why we feel lonely. After all, that feeling is generated in the mind, so we have the answer somewhere in there; we simply need to pinpoint the root cause. Sometimes that requires a deep dive into the subconscious to extract the information from repressed memories. (This is where a licensed professional may be able to help.) It is frightening to feel lonely and have no idea why. Negative emotions are like an infection waiting to spread throughout our minds, bodies, and environment. Loneliness can easily lead to sepsis of the mind. If not handled properly, a negative response could trigger other negative emotions, causing a whirlwind of negative thoughts that lead to a sharp decrease in quality of life. We need healthy ways to acknowledge and cope with feelings of loneliness.

One helpful method is to change our perception of what it means to be lonely. From the pillars of self-centeredness, the first of the five, humility, can be a useful tool. Humility allows us to acknowledge our flaws while simultaneously understanding that every other person in the world has them too. The irony here is we are not alone in feeling lonely. If we understand this, we can see this scenario defies the definition of loneliness. There truly is strength in numbers, so we must not be afraid to reach out by whatever means to find others afflicted with similar struggles. A great place to learn healthy coping skills is through someone who has successfully navigated a similar trial.

While it is nice to find someone to relate to when experiencing a negative emotion, that is not the only effective coping strategy. Human interaction with someone willing to listen without judgment is often enough to take our mind off feeling alone. A second way humility can aid in our fight against feeling lonely is in understanding that discovering why we feel alone and what to do about it might be over our heads. We do not have all the answers, and that is okay. The need for help does not make us weak or incompetent. It makes us human. There are a lot of people on the planet; somebody out there has the answers we need. Seeking counsel is sometimes imperative.

I mentioned the value of therapy previously. Mental health professionals are gifted at getting us to look at a situation in a different way, leading us to new and improved thought processes that ultimately alter the way we think and behave. In most cases, when we attempt to change the way we feel, we have to change what we are doing. This is where resilience comes into play.

In addition to reaching out to those who share our negative feelings or therapists who can help us cope with those negative feelings, forming a positive bond might be the solution to combating loneliness. We can reach out to someone with similar passions, hobbies, or interests. Sharing commonalities appeals to our sense of belonging, which humans crave. It fulfills a need to evolve in our personal development as we strive for self-centeredness.

We must own our feelings. It is up to us to decide how long we will allow loneliness to endure. Though we may feel isolated by our thoughts and emotions, we are not alone in the slightest. We must recruit the help or the company we need from the resources around us and let the feeling of loneliness dissipate from our mind. We replace it with feelings of fulfillment and accomplishment because we know we are responsible for taking control of our life, and in choosing how we behave, our feelings change.

◆ ◆ ◆

NAVIGATING DEPRESSION

> The most important decision you make is to be in a good mood.
> —Attributed to Voltaire

One of the major drawbacks to loneliness is the possibility of it spiraling into depression. A simple definition for depression is a state of feeling sad, having low spirits, or a melancholy disposition. From a mental health perspective, depression is a mental disorder that affects mood and perpetuates disinterest in life events and even basic survival activities such as eating, sleeping, waking up, personal care, and companionship.

There are two distinct categories of depression: clinical and regular. Clinical depression is the most severe of the two.

♦ CLINICAL DEPRESSION

The standard label for clinical depression is "major depressive disorder," meaning a severely negative state of mind that can threaten the will to live. The self-centered approach recognizes the need for a team to combat clinical depression. It takes humility to recognize that this situation cannot be faced alone. If we are unable to make this assertion ourselves, we can only hope someone in our life cares enough to get us the aid we need. I believe very strongly in the power of the mind, but when the mind itself betrays us and tries to lead us astray, we need to enlist help from family, friends, life coaches, psychologists, and psychiatrists to keep us tethered to reality.

As I stated earlier, I am not a professional therapist, so my recommendation here is to seek out a mental health expert who specializes in depression. It is important to seek someone competent, trustworthy, and passionate about their profession. It is also essential to select a therapist we can build a rapport with and who makes us feel comfortable—someone who makes us feel like our well-being is the primary goal of the meetings. A strong bond with a mental health professional with an intellectual understanding of what we are going through is an effective way to fight clinical depression. Their understanding leads to effective treatment plans and activities for us to engage in to help us live a happier life.

◆ REGULAR DEPRESSION

The second type of depression is regular depression. This is a common disorder experienced for varied reasons. If not dealt with, it can evolve into clinical depression. This type of depression is dangerous because it typically results from a traumatic or adverse life event, and we experience many of these over a lifetime, ranging from appalling to mild. Being a victim of a sex crime or abuse of some sort, seeing military combat, losing a loved one, performing poorly at work or school, being rejected, and feeling inadequate are just a few of thousands of events we might encounter.

If we struggle with regular depression, I believe the best coping strategy begins with making a list of people and activities in life that don't suck when we are not feeling depressed. This way, when depression strikes, we have a personalized list of coping strategies to deploy. I believe strongly in communication. Even if we do not want to talk to anyone, I find that I always feel better after I communicate with someone I trust. Luckily, I have several family members and friends to turn to in my times of need. I feel fortunate that my wife, the person I spend the most time with, is at the top of that list.

Unfortunately, the toughest part of communicating our depression is finding a person we can count on almost all the time. No matter how bad we feel, the right person will rarely make us feel worse, and the conversation will not annoy us. Sometimes we need someone to listen to us vent or rant, and the right person will know what we need in that moment. Use your humility and seek the comfort of someone who has earned your trust in situations like this. Keep in mind, this trustworthy individual is likely a family member or friend, not a licensed therapist. It would be risky to expect this person to help you feel better 100 percent of the time.

If we really do not need to talk to anyone, we can stimulate our body or mind. The number one strategy is exercise. I am a huge advocate for the benefits of working out. Exercise provides biological effects that stimulate the areas of the mind responsible for depression. We are defying the emotion of depression by forcing the negative symptoms out and replacing them with a chemical reaction that produces feelings opposite of depression. This is why it is so important to remember the power we have to decide how we want to feel.

When I decide not to stay in a state of depression, another staple of my coping mechanisms is comedy. Some believe the saying about laughter being the best medicine originated from a Bible verse: Proverbs 17:22, "A cheerful heart is good medicine."

If ever I am feeling down, I prefer stand-up comedy over funny movies. I cannot tell you how appreciative I am of people like Steve Harvey, Dave Chappelle, Kevin Hart, and Jerry Seinfeld. Humor causes the ultimate shift in perspective for me. Comedians joke about real-life events and sometimes make light of profoundly serious situations, which is a reminder not to look at the world through a single lens. There might not always be a lighter side, but there is bound to be a perspective that is not wholly negative.

A huge shout-out to all comedians for their ability to make us laugh. Whether they realize it or not, they are instrumental in keeping my mental health in a positive space, and I am grateful for what they do.

If you don't have a sense of humor, first of all, my heart goes out to you. Secondly, what comedy does for me, your passion can do for you. If you are into cars, sports, reality TV, nature, history, gardening, or whatever else, there is a channel to watch or an article to read that can help you feel fulfilled instead of empty, happy instead of sad. The self-centered person recognizes when a state of depression sets in and chooses not to let that feeling fester. They recognize the need for joy and laughter to balance out negative emotions, and they take the actions necessary to create that balance.

◆ ◆ ◆

NAVIGATING ANGER

> Every day we have plenty of opportunities to get angry, stressed or offended. But what you're doing when you indulge these negative emotions is giving something outside yourself power over your happiness. You can choose to not let little things upset you.
>
> —**Joel Osteen**

Another emotion leading to negative thoughts and potentially destructive behavior is anger. This particular emotion is especially dangerous because it seems to spark the most instinctive and impulsive behaviors. Anger allows for almost no processing time, so before we know it, we have said or done something that might be difficult to apologize for and move on from. The chemical reaction in the brain when angry can lead to long-term physiological health concerns such as high blood pressure and clogged arteries, which of course increase the risk of heart disease. This is an extreme case, but it provides context for how serious allowing our anger to rage out of control on a regular basis can be. If someone you know has a resting heart rate of 500 and walks around with their metaphorical body temperature gauge permanently stuck in the red, they are potentially overheating their vessel to the point of heart failure.

I have a love-hate relationship with anger because I do not view it as a constant negative. Since I have taken the time to know myself, I understand that if I am truly angry, I am temporarily motivated and energized to achieve whatever short-term goal I can set on short notice. The boost of adrenaline and laser focus I gain is pretty amazing. Achieving this state feels like an out-of-body experience, in a good way. I received the most benefit from my anger during my days as an athlete, but my wife has also witnessed some tasks around the house getting completed when I feel upset!

As I've gotten older, I have less use for anger. Now I allow it to manifest only if I have a way to channel it into productive behavior. In nine out of ten situations, nothing positive will emerge from me staying angry, so I decide not to do so. Remember, anger is an emotion, so we cannot prevent the onset of it. We can, however, make it a goal not to stay angry once we have experienced an unpleasant event.

This is one of those times where the phrase "Easier said than done" applies perfectly. I believe anger is the most readily available emotion out of all of them. In my case, it is quite easy to get upset when I feel mistreated, disrespected, or attacked verbally or physically. If I had a default setting for potentially destructive emotions, anger would be the one my brain chooses. For anyone who struggles with anger or knows someone who does, here are a couple of suggestions for how a self-centered person might cope with it in a healthy and productive way.

When dealing with interpersonal conflict, humility will play a role because it allows us to process a situation in real time from the other person's point of view. We recognize anger as an impulse emotion that all humans possess as a part of our genetic code, and we make an effort to separate the emotion from the person. Detaching the emotion from the source makes it easier to process because it becomes less personal. We can then avoid taking anger personally and better understand what the angry person is trying to communicate rather than focusing on the angry demeanor. This keeps us rational instead of intent on matching angry energy.

Think about it. We do not get mad and have the urge to retaliate against anger itself; that would be pointless. We get mad at the angry person for how poorly they might be handling themselves in the moment. If we stay focused on a resolution, we can keep ourselves centered and control the conflict. Resilience is also important in this case because that is how we keep our mind on what matters instead of irrational words and actions. When people get angry, they are no longer in a rational state. They might yell, scream, use profanity, berate, belittle, and make every effort to make us angry or hurt our feelings to drag us into a fight. Resilience helps us resist the urge to engage in negative behavior and wade through all that nonsense, thereby keeping us focused on a solution that will end the conflict.

The easy action would be to match the tone and disrespect we are receiving because that is a natural response for someone with self-respect. Lord knows we have to let these people know we are not to be disrespected, and what better way to express that than by shouting our displeasure at someone, degrading them, or threatening them?

Try to recall a time in your life when you said something or behaved in a way you regret because you were angry at the time. Now replay that situation in your mind and think of how you would handle it if you could do it over. If you came up with a different strategy than the one you used in the moment, there is hope for you in controlling your behavior when getting angry in the future. Even in the moment, you can think about the cause of the conflict and remain focused on the actual issue as opposed to the emotion involved. Being angry distracts us from what we are trying to accomplish.

How many times have you been in a fight with someone, and by the time the fight is over, you can't even recall what started the fight because you've ended up in a place that has nothing at all to do with the catalyst? In my case, plenty! The self-centered person combats anger with a peaceful purpose. People, without conscious effort, tend to mimic one another. If we control our anger and communicate calmly with a purpose, it's surprising how often we will get that in return. Whomever we are arguing with will likely recognize how our calm demeanor illuminates their irrational behavior. Self-preservation is always in play with our psyche, and nobody wants to be the only person yelling and screaming in a fight. It's not a good look, so they will hopefully stop behaving that way.

For those of us who deal with people who are relentless in their barrage of insults and personal attacks in order to get us to engage in conflict, remember what we control and what we don't—or in this case, *who* we don't control. We have absolutely no control over what other people might do or say. We must hold ourselves accountable to the standard of behavior we set for ourselves and not allow someone else's anger to influence our behavior. Stay true to yourself, and eventually these people will understand it is pointless to try to fight with you.

For those of us who get angry when bad luck strikes, even for trivial things, the self-centered perspective guides us to take a similar approach to dealing with angry people and focus on the solution to the problem rather than the problem itself. We already know the source of our anger, so there is no need to harp on that detail. What we need is for that issue to go away, so we must direct all our energy toward a solution.

Whether it's car trouble, spilled coffee on our nice clothes, dropping and subsequently cracking our cell phone screen, or getting a crease in our new shoes, there will be hell to pay in the mind of an angry person. There are countless other scenarios in which we might get angry, but I want us to consider how being angry will benefit us or anyone else in these situations. If there is a purpose for our anger that will aid us in fixing our problem, by all means, we should use that anger to power our solution. But if there is no practical application, we must use that energy to find the solution, leave our anger with the problem, and move on.

It is not healthy to keep anger stored; if we harbor it, there is a good chance that anger will be released in a way that hurts us or someone close to us. Our anger often affects our behavior and how we interact with other people. Angry communication is toxic, and the people we communicate with in anger will take our negativity and spread it to the next person they interact with, and so on. Who knows how many people could end up having unpleasant interactions based on an event that started with a cup of coffee?

We must find a solution to the problem and leave the anger right there in the moment instead of dragging it around to poison everything we come into contact with.

◆ ◆ ◆

NAVIGATING FEAR

> No power so effectually robs the mind of all its powers of acting and reasoning as fear.
> —**Attributed to Edmund Burke**

If there are a "big three" of emotions that have the most potential to prevent us from being fulfilled in life, achieving success, and behaving in a way we are proud of, I believe they would be stress, depression, and anger. But fear also belongs on that list.

Fear, much like stress and anger, is not a totally negative emotion. In its proper perspective, fear keeps us safe from physical dangers and protects our psychological well-being from negative emotions. Here are a few quick examples.

Based on fear, we would be reluctant to walk across a freeway where vehicles are traveling 65 to 75 mph. Fear alerts our mind that this is a perilous action and that being struck by a vehicle traveling at that speed will not end well for us. Fear keeps us safe from engaging in an act that puts our life at unnecessary risk. Psychologically, fear can also protect us from many different negative feelings, such as rejection, sadness, and embarrassment, to name a few. Take a wedding reception scenario. Everyone reports to the dance floor per the DJ's request—except for us because our fear of being judged and ridiculed reminds us that we have no rhythm. The safest action in this situation is to not report to the dance floor. By remaining seated, we can leave this event with our dignity still intact.

From these scenarios, it is easy to see fear can be helpful and sometimes necessary in protecting our life and self-esteem. But fear becomes a negative issue we must overcome when it impedes our ability to be ourselves, act, or find joy.

These roadblocks suggest there are different types of fear. A few common types we as people must conquer to increase our quality of life are the fear of being judged or cast out; the fear of failure; and tangible fears. These types of fear can have a devastating impact if we do not challenge them. Fear might be one of the most powerful emotions, but we must remember it is only an emotion. Emotions are not meant to last forever. They are temporary and should not be granted the power of governing life choices. With this understanding, we can put fear in its proper perspective and navigate it using the self-centered perspective.

◆ FEAR OF JUDGMENT

One of the most glaring deficiencies in our genetic makeup is our fundamental need to fit in. Our willingness to conform to the rules and behaviors established by whatever environment we seek to be a part of confirms a flaw in the human condition and our need to feel connected and accepted. Society plays a huge role in perpetuating fear because societal norms set the standard for acceptable and unacceptable behavior. We are sometimes reluctant to be our authentic self for fear of being made to feel as though we do not have a place in society.

I understand the compulsion to avoid being categorized as a pariah, but conformity still sabotages our quality of life. The irony of living a life pretending to be someone we are not in order to feel connected is we still end up feeling alone. We have nothing in common with those we pretend to relate to; therefore, our life is often full of negative emotions, such as emptiness, shame, and regret. I also understand the need for conforming as it pertains to specific environments. When we are at home or with friends, we are more likely to be ourselves due to the established comfortability. At work, we must be a little more professional with our language and interactions. At church, we tend to be more respectful of people and the proceedings. At a concert, we may unleash a wilder side we keep suppressed under most circumstances. Point being, we sometimes must adjust our behavior to fit the environment we are in.

As a self-centered individual, however, the only conforming necessary involves making sure our behaviors line up with the core principles we have set for ourselves. We never conform strictly for the approval or acceptance of others, and the principles by which we live will be suitable for any environment with minimal adjustment.

When I think about fear of judgment, the group that jumps to the forefront of my mind is the LGBTQ community. I can't think of a group of people judged more harshly than those whose sexual orientation does not match the societal norm. Although strides have been made in the direction of acceptance and respect for all people, members of this community are still fearful at times of being completely open about their sexuality. They wish to avoid mean-spirited comments or professional discrimination.

The self-centered perspective breaks down this scenario as follows. Is it fair for a group of people to be mistreated, devalued as humans, slandered, and overlooked based on their preference in significant other? Of course it isn't fair. Unfairness is a fundamental quality of the world. The question to ask is, is this type of judgmental scrutiny wrong? The answer of course is yes.

When confronted with behavior that is objectively wrong, the self-centered principal pillars sustain us to do what is suited to our psychological well-being. Humility allows us to recognize flaws in the thinking of others. In this case, we turn the tables on those seeking to demean by showing compassion for their ignorance. Deficient knowledge and understanding runs rampant in society today, and we are all guilty of this condition to some degree. We understand the hurtful remarks and cruelty toward this community are in some cases based on a lack of a desire to be enlightened and informed. Because we are unable to forcibly open the minds of those who wish to remain close minded, all we can do is live in a way that proves different lifestyle choice is not synonymous with wrong or offensive. We do not have to share the same taste in life partners to be good people.

If we are resilient in the face of unjust scrutiny and ridicule, exhibit kindness, manifest genuine efficacy and complete confidence in who we are and what we represent, and are unfazed by what others think, we are well on our way to fulfilling the vision Dr. Martin Luther King Jr. shared in his famous "I Have a Dream" speech. If we consistently make good choices and treat people with respect, we bring value to the human race based on the content of our character and not our sexual orientation.

When we hide who we are for fear of being tagged "abnormal," we surrender our power to govern our actions and live a happier life. Feeling forced to conform drains the quality of life and pushes our negative emotions to the forefront of our mind. It is imperative to take the time to examine what we are doing to ourselves when we allow the fear of being judged to guide our behavior. We are essentially telling the world, "I'm not quite mentally strong enough to establish principles to live by, make my own decisions, and stand by my actions. I can't have an identity of my own because it wouldn't be accepted, so I must do whatever the world thinks I should do and be whatever the world thinks I should be."

If we enjoyed being told what to do, what to think, and given an identity to adhere to, then conforming to societal demands would not be an issue for us. However, if we do not like being told what to do, society becomes a tyrant attempting to enslave our individuality and our quality of life. Revisiting slavery in any form is unacceptable for a person who values their freedom to choose. As long as we try to be the best version of ourselves every day, fear can be mitigated.

⬥ FEAR OF FAILURE

The fear of failure is a psychological dead-end that many of us accept as absolute. If we examine this fear closely, I believe we can conclude it is an illusion. Failing is not what we are afraid of; we fear the negative thoughts and beliefs generated by being unsuccessful in an endeavor. We may experience embarrassment, shame, inadequacy, and vulnerability. We sometimes associate our self-worth with perceived failure by making statements like "I'm a failure." But by now we know that perspective comes from possessing a sensitive id and must be reevaluated using the self-centered perspective.

First, we must examine the source of the negative feelings associated with failure. If we want to learn how to boot scootin' boogie, salsa, or Dougie, we might get discouraged at times, but we would likely not have deep-rooted negative feelings if we were alone with our efforts. The issue arises if someone witnesses those clumsy convulsions we call dancing. Now the humiliation and embarrassment set in, and self-esteem drops. What we must realize is those negative feelings that seem to come from our mind actually come from an external source. We're not afraid to fail when trying something new. We're afraid of how someone else will make us feel if we fail at trying something new.

The self-centered perspective can help eliminate that feeling with two of the five pillars. Our humility should comfort us with our shortcomings. By understanding there is room for growth in every aspect of our life, we see there is no need to fear failing or what other people might think or say. We must not miss opportunities to enrich our life based on unsubstantiated fear. Failure is not to be feared; it is to be relentlessly challenged until it becomes a learning experience in our story of achievement.

This leads to the second pillar that will aid us in navigating the fear of failure. Not only must we examine the negative feelings associated with failing, but we must also define what failure means to us. Resilience can put the subject of failure into perspective. Going back to learning how to perform different dances, if we've never attempted the dances before and weren't born with the natural talent, grace, dexterity, and aptitude for learning, it might be a struggle to master them. Our first attempt might be a total disaster. We might say to ourselves, "This is impossible. I don't know how people coordinate their movements to the beat of a song, and I don't know how people can move their bodies in certain ways. Are their muscles made out of rubber? Do they not have bones? Because I do, and they seem to be getting in the way of my progress!"

If learning these dance moves is something we want to master, then being resilient will transform our view of failure. That first day was not a failure. It was only the start of the learning process. When we are resilient, we don't stop working until the process is complete. The process is complete when we can lead the herd in boot scootin' boogieing on our next line-dancing excursion. The time frame is irrelevant. The point is, we never acknowledge failure when learning those dances. Each practice session is a part of the learning process. We can only fail if we quit. If we keep our fear of failure in the proper perspective, we see that notion for the farce it is. The only thing to fear is regression or stagnation of our personal growth . . . and snakes. It's definitely okay to fear snakes.

◆ TANGIBLE FEARS

One of the most common types of fear is tangible fear, which, as humans, we all likely share in one way or another. We might be afraid of certain people, death, animals (snakes), heights, darkness, flying in an airplane, or, the worst-case scenario, snakes on a plane! I won't spend too much time focusing on these types of fears because for the most part, this is an aspect of life where I condone avoidance. Simply staying away from these fears will not harm our growth as a person. If we are afraid of death, I don't believe Russian roulette is the best exercise to "get over it." If we are deathly afraid of snakes, I would not suggest a stroll through a snake pit to "face our fears." There is a better chance of cardiac arrest than overcoming our thanatophobia or ophidiophobia using those techniques.

However, if we believe a tangible fear is holding us back from experiencing a higher quality of life and we wish to overcome that fear, resilience is going to be our guide. Attempting to change a behavior or mitigate a fear response to a particular stimulus involves goal setting, an altered perspective, and practice. If we set a goal to overcome our fear of heights, we need to put that goal in a less terrifying perspective. We have to question what exactly makes us fearful of being high off the ground. Is it truly the height, or are we afraid of falling from a high place? Does the lack of stability of whatever we are standing on when in an elevated position scare us? Does the view looking down from a high vantage point spark our discomfort? Those are different from being afraid of heights. When we discover what causes the fear, we can craft a solution that will eliminate it or at least make it manageable.

❖ ❖ ❖

NAVIGATING LOW SELF-ESTEEM

> If we get our self-esteem from superficial places, from our popularity, appearance, business success, financial situation, health, any of these, we will be disappointed, because no one can guarantee that we'll have them tomorrow.
>
> —**Kathy Ireland**

Low self-esteem is a tricky feeling because it involves how we see ourselves. Supposedly self-esteem is how comfortable and confident we are in our own skin and the value we place on our personal existence—meaning all these thoughts are being manifested internally by our brain. I say supposedly because it is my belief that if a person has low self-esteem, their opinion of themselves does not originate from their own beliefs. Thoughts that suggest "I'm not good enough," "I'm not attractive enough," or "I'm not rich enough" or reflect the impression we are defined by our physical, emotional, and personality flaws are rooted in an external standard of success, beauty, wealth, happiness, and other constructs. Guess who developed these societal norms we've decided to measure our self-worth against? People!

People decided what it means for all of us to live a successful life. People decided what it means to be attractive. People decided what it means to be intelligent. For whatever reason, as individuals we started measuring ourselves and comparing ourselves to those standards and other people who appear to meet or exceed the standard. If we fall short in some areas, we feel inadequate, and that feeling affects our self-esteem. Low self-esteem is a prevalent mental health issue that I would like to see wiped off the face of the earth; and I believe it to be the easiest negative feeling to overcome because it is the simplest feeling to understand.

To effectively cope with low self-esteem, the self-centered perspective calls on our understanding of humility and efficacy. Humility helps us recognize our flaws and keep our attributes in the right perspective. This is human nature in a nutshell. We all have positive attributes, and we all have flaws. The people who developed these standards we live by are flawed just like we are. Why on earth would I allow another flawed human being to define my self-image? Answer: I would not. Why on earth would I allow another flawed human being to define success for my life? Answer: I would not.

Our circumstances are unique to us. If we earn a six- or seven-figure income, many people would say we are rich. If we have earned $25,000 a year for ten years and suddenly in year eleven we earn $50,000, we may feel just as rich and successful as a millionaire. Will we be sharing a hotel floor with Jay-Z and Beyoncé at the Ritz on that salary? Probably not, but it is still twice as much as we were accustomed to living on. Let's imagine the peace of mind and feeling of accomplishment that comes from knowing we can afford groceries when we need them and pay our bills on time. Our self-esteem should be in a healthy place.

Our personal circumstances are the only variables to consider when we conduct a self-assessment. We must stop comparing our bank account to Taylor Swift's and focus on what we are doing or can do with our life as opposed to feeling inadequate because Taylor's bank account has significantly more zeroes at the end than ours.

Consider what we have come to value as a species. I am in no way hating on the money that entertainers and professional athletes make because they earn every cent of their income based on our interests. However, if I had to get real and put a value on assets we have as humans, I think the people with the aptitude to become doctors to heal us, people who put themselves in harm's way to protect us, or a really good therapist or teacher who helps us strengthen our mind possess the attributes that I personally hold in high regard. If I am experiencing unusual chest pains, I need a cardiologist, not LeBron James. In fact, as revered as LeBron is for his immense basketball talent, he would need that same cardiologist if his ticker were acting up.

We all need the type of people who get fulfillment by helping others. The disparity in monetary earnings when assessing the incomes of people who save, protect, and change lives versus those who shoot three-pointers, hit home runs, and throw touchdown passes is staggering. The people who decided this makes sense are the same people trying to dictate how we see ourselves. Think about what happened to society when Major League Baseball went on strike back in the '90s and canceled a bunch of games, including the World Series. Sure, it was disappointing for sports fans, but those of us who were alive managed to get through it okay. Imagine the societal impact of all medical professionals going on strike for nine months. No hospitals, no surgeries, no medication. Can you imagine how many lives might be lost? There would be devastating consequences for many people.

We must think for ourselves and recognize that our value as a human is equal to that of anyone with incredible talents, beauty, or athletic ability. Most of those attributes are superficial and temporary, and how we measure ourselves should run so much deeper than the surface. We are the masters of our domain. We are only accountable to the personal standards set by the person in the mirror. We need to set our own bar for success or failure based on our circumstances rather than on social norms created by people just as flawed as us.

CHAPTER 12

NAVIGATING DIFFICULT EXTERNAL LIFE EXPERIENCES

We are all on a different life journey to the same final destination: death. Because that last stop is random, we should make plenty of meaningful stops along the way—being who we want to be, doing what we want to do, and appreciating those traveling with us so we may find daily fulfillment and not be left with assumptions, questions, and regret.

◆ ◆ ◆

THE TRAGEDY OF DEATH

One of life's toughest challenges is figuring out how to cope with death. Although we understand that our time on earth is temporary and our lives as well as the lives of those we cherish will ultimately come to an end, that knowledge does not provide comfort when we are faced with it.

Death has no bias and can strike without warning. We often do not have the opportunity to prepare. I believe the reason we have such a difficult time coping with death is that we try not to focus on it without cause. Think about the difference between coping with a death you are prepared for and one that occurs suddenly. If someone is terminally ill, a known chronic substance abuser, or advanced in age, to some degree we have been preparing for that person's departure; we know it's coming. When that unfortunate day happens, it is typically not as devastating to our emotions as someone who was just "running to the store" and never returned home. Because we are psychologically prepared to cope with an anticipated loss, the healing process starts well in advance of the actual terrible event.

I contend that we should allow humility to drive our mindfulness of mortality. If we understand that untimely deaths can happen to anyone at any time, we need to make room in our minds for that perspective alongside our preoccupation with day-to-day activities that lull us into a "this could never happen to me" point of view. By keeping ourselves aware, we mitigate the paralyzing shock and are better able to cope and grieve. The awareness that people (or pets) we love, rely on, and spend quality time with can be gone from our lives in an instant shapes a new perspective.

It is dangerous to our health and state of mind to become overly dependent on the presence of others in our lives. Family members and great friends who are always there for us make it easy to feel like our very existence is tied to the lives of other people. Each of us has value to humanity. Every one of us has the power to add kindness, love, positivity, patience, understanding, protection, advice, forgiveness, or any number of acts and traits that promote peace in our world. Deep connections with our loved ones are certainly a valid goal and source of joy, but while those connections enhance our quality of life, they do not define our existence.

When we lose someone close to us, a period of sorrow, grief, loneliness, or anger is expected. Missing the physical presence of a loved one is natural. In due time, we must try to remember that the lack of physical presence is not the same as a complete lack of presence. I believe the best way to cope with losing a loved one is to carry on that person's spirit.

One suggestion for how to go about doing that is to avoid isolating ourselves with negative feelings. We must try not to push away people who want to be there for us. Regarding emotional and mental well-being, there is strength in numbers. External support can help us navigate this incredibly difficult time. Also, remembering how our lost loved one was always there for us when we needed them can inspire us to carry on that spirit by doing for others what that person did for us, continuing their legacy. We of all people can appreciate how much value that adds to the life of a person in need.

Losing someone dear to us can cause the mind to race with thoughts of how much our lives have changed. These thoughts raise stress and anxiety levels and can lead to feeling completely lost in life. Engaging our mind with something productive that incorporates the memories of our lost loved one can help. Starting a charity in their name, making a social statement, or raising awareness on a topic dear to our loved one will give us purpose and keep the mind occupied with healthy thoughts while simultaneously honoring our loved ones.

Another suggestion, on a more superficial level, is to acquire some keepsake that represents our loved one and our relationship, whether it be jewelry, a T-shirt, a bumper sticker, a tattoo, or anything tangible that reminds us that our loved one is always with us in spirit. We will carry on everything good they represented. Spirit keepsakes can aid with feelings of loneliness. Our bodies are fragile. Even the strongest of us will eventually weaken. Our insides break down slowly but surely, and our mortal bodies perish. Our legacies, however, have an opportunity to achieve immortality. That is what we need to do for our lost loved ones. If we remember them by passing on their spirit to others, that cycle could continue until the end of the earth.

Death is a part of life that will knock us down. Getting knocked down is, quite frankly, expected. When we are down, we need psychological tools at the ready to get back up and experience a high quality of life. We can be better prepared emotionally for untimely deaths by taking full advantage of the time we have together and by being grateful and appreciative in the moment so at the very least we are not left with regrets that might deepen the negative feelings already associated with losing someone. Resilience is key. We must wade through some murky, deep, and tumultuous emotional waters to act despite the circumstances that make us want to give up.

If we lose someone close to us, we must live on and be on the lookout for situations that remind us of that person. We must seize every opportunity to act on their behalf. That is how that person's spirit remains alive within us.

◆ ◆ ◆

NAVIGATING ILLNESSES AND DISABILITIES

Chronic illness and genetic defects are unfortunate elements of life. Much of the time, we are born with these illnesses, which plants them firmly in the category of elements we do not control. As we have learned, there is little point in fretting over circumstances we have no control over. All we can do is focus on a solution—or, in the case of some illnesses, disabilities, and disorders, a suitable coping strategy.

Living life with an uncontrollable diagnosis from birth is slightly different from living with an illness that develops over time. My opinion could be off base, but I believe that those born with this type of disability are naturally resilient. They must adapt to their unique circumstances to survive and thrive in the world same as everyone else, yet without the advantage of a healthy birth. The world is cruel and relentless to everyone without bias, so to be given a handicap from the very beginning is a punch to the gut nobody deserves.

Earlier in this book, we came to understand life is not fair. The self-centered perspective recognizes the uncontrollable nature of this situation, effectively eliminating the tendency to feel "different" or harbor negative feelings toward the congenital disability itself or people born without the disability. None of us are born with the same DNA, so in essence, we are all outliers. The one person we should always count on for support is ourselves. We tell ourselves, "This is the hand I was dealt. I did not choose this. This does not define me. I am defined by the thoughts I turn into actions and the actions I turn into accomplishments." The self-centered perspective allows us the clarity to see that a healthy mind allows us to play any hand and be successful despite the obstacles put in our path.

◆ ◆ ◆

NAVIGATING PSYCHOLOGICAL DISORDERS

An area of life I have personal experience in is psychological disorders. There are hundreds of different disorders, and each one presents a unique set of challenges for the individual experiencing the disorder and for the people around that individual. My understanding and support go out to every single person afflicted with a psychological hardship.

Negative feelings often come along with any disorder—depression, loneliness, fear, desperation, hopelessness, and numbness, to name just a few we might experience. Those feelings do not define us, nor will they govern our actions if we focus on the power of perspective and choices. I have never personally been diagnosed with a psychological disorder, but I am very close to people who have been diagnosed. From my experience as a person aspiring to be self-centered, a humble approach serves me well when interacting with these individuals because it allows me to see situations from their perspective. It is imperative to get the person with the diagnosis to understand that they are not their diagnosis.

The first step in developing healthy coping strategies is to separate the person from the symptoms. We hear it all the time: "I'm depressed," "I'm bipolar," "I'm bulimic," or "I'm OCD." These are situations where people literally refer to themselves as the disorder itself! If I were to put myself in the shoes of someone with a disorder, my perspective would go something like this: "I'm Ray. I have been diagnosed with a disorder that is attempting to make my mind work against me. The diagnosis is an external influence separate from my actual state of being. It's my mind, and I'm the only one who controls it. When something like a disorder tries to get me to surrender my thoughts, feelings, and behaviors to it, I understand that I can choose to say no. I may not be able to control my thoughts and emotions, but I understand that no human can.

"What I can control is the duration of those thoughts, putting those thoughts in the proper perspective for my mental health, and my actions in response to external forces trying to dictate my mood and behavior. I am simply dealing with my unique circumstances and figuring out how to navigate the pros and cons of my DNA and environment. I know everyone faces the ups and downs of the human condition, and all humans are the same from that vantage point. Our pros and cons may differ, but we all have them. My normal is different from the next person's. So, when someone asks, 'What's wrong with you?' my answer would be, 'The same thing that's wrong with you; I'm human.' This is the hand I was dealt, and I'll play it. I'm Ray, and I am not my diagnosis."

While metaphorically putting myself in someone else's shoes helps me better understand their perspective, it is not beneficial to that person if my understanding doesn't lead to the ability to help alleviate some of the negative feelings associated with being diagnosed with a psychological disorder. As I mentioned before, I have insight into the lives of two people, one male and one female, who have been diagnosed with psychological disabilities, and they happen to be two of my children. I will share some of the relevant details of their stories now.

My son's story is an excellent reminder of how unpredictable life can be. From birth to preteen, I would describe him as one of the happiest kids in the world. He never had an unkind word for anyone, and he was very caring, playful, and always had a smile on his face. During that time, he was my reminder of what stress-free looked like. He offered an alternative perspective to an adult life saddled with worry, responsibility, and what felt like nonstop personal sacrifice. As parents and adults, we allow ourselves to be consumed by all the things we have to get done. We forget life can provide joy, peace of mind, and personal fulfillment on the other side of our obligations.

In 2010, my son fell off a bicycle, hitting his head on a concrete curb and losing consciousness briefly. He suffered a TBI (traumatic brain injury). Physically, he appeared to be okay once he regained consciousness, but the next day, he had his first seizure. Needless to say, this was a scary time for our family because we had no experience with seizures, and we had no idea what was wrong.

Naturally, we took him to a doctor, but there was no consensus on what caused the seizure. I will spare you the details of this situation over the next eleven years, but here's the summation: there were many seizures; there were many trips to hospitals and to many different specialists; many tests were conducted; many different seizure medications were administered; there were many trips in emergency vehicles; there were many moments of uncertainty. You notice what was sparse during all this? Answers! In over eleven years, we never received a clear diagnosis of what happened to our son when he fell off that bike.

In growing up and attempting to become a functional member of society, he has encountered hardship after hardship. Without a comprehensive treatment plan, living with unexplained seizures became our normal. This normal became synonymous with constant struggle. He struggled with school, sports, relationships, steady employment, and mood stability. Finally, in year twelve, he received a diagnosis the DSM-5 (Diagnostic and Statistical Manual of Mental Disorders) refers to as PNES (psychogenic nonepileptic seizures). In my son's case, this means he will have what appears to be an epileptic seizure when his stress level is too high. His seizures occur based on psychological distress instead of abnormal brain activity, which is the case with epilepsy. With an understanding in place, we could now begin to overcome this obstacle.

Over the years, I got caught up in caring for him and responding to emergencies. Constantly worrying about his health and state of mind, I lost sight of the saddest element of this story. The happy-go-lucky kid who reminded me life is as fun as you make it was gone. It did not register for me when he became quick tempered and moody, walking around with an unhappy disposition. He transformed into the complete opposite of his nature as a young child, angry that the outside world doesn't want to understand his plight or offer the tiniest sliver of compassion for his unfortunate circumstances. He feels like the bike accident is the cause of everything that has not gone according to his plans, which frustrates him greatly.

This feeling is natural and valid because that event left us all in a state of what-if. What if he never fell off that bike and hit his head? What would his life be like? While those questions are great for deep thinking, they are not useful for developing healthy coping strategies for an issue.

Because the diagnosis is a new development, the self-centered process is just beginning for him. He is currently processing PNES as an obstacle he needs to overcome and not a fixed part of who he is. For eleven years, this condition has defined him. The decisions he has made to this point reflect a person just trying to cope with a hardship with no solution, without giving serious consideration to whether those coping techniques and behaviors were in his own best interest. He now realizes that focusing internally and taking control of his perspective is the key to a less stressful life. Less stress means fewer seizures. Fewer seizures will boost his efficacy and give him the confidence he needs to pursue his goals without the fear of his health sabotaging his life.

I don't know if I will ever see that joyful and playful kid again, but I know if he continues to take the time to understand what he needs to keep himself balanced while navigating his unique life circumstances, he has it in him to be happy and impact those around him in a positive way.

My daughter has been diagnosed with bipolar II disorder, which essentially means a person suffers from drastic mood swings ranging from the pinnacle of euphoria to the deepest, darkest depths of despair, sometimes for reasons unknown. As if that weren't enough to deal with, a bipolar episode can strike at any moment and last for an indiscriminate amount of time. It could be an hour, a day, a week, or even a month. It is an exceptionally high psychological hurdle, and it is quite common in the United States; millions of people have to contend with this mental hardship.

My daughter is a very private person, so I'm going to share a little bit about her story from the perspective of a parent and avoid going into detail on specific events in her journey. I want to preface this summary of the experience my wife and I shared in being the parents of a child with this disorder by stating that the disorder was extremely difficult for us to cope with. You might wonder, "Why was it so difficult for you and your wife? Your daughter was diagnosed, not the two of you." That is a very fair point, and in no way am I comparing our struggles with those of my daughter, who battles this hardship in her mind every day.

What I've learned about bipolar disorder is it doesn't just impact the individual. The collateral damage to loved ones is as real an issue as the disorder itself. Because we love our daughter tremendously, her pain and suffering are our pain and suffering. From our perspective, it felt as though we were diagnosed as well. We went through emotional highs and lows, but in a different way. We experienced uncertainty in a different way. We experienced negative thoughts in a different way—the difference being that as a parent, it is heartbreaking to see our children struggle.

My wife and I shared many moments of pure fear, worry, and panic because we did not have a solution for the problem and were uncertain there even was one. It was terrifying to feel helpless when it was obvious our child needed help. Many restless and sleepless nights were spent being concerned for her well-being and trying to figure out how to help our daughter simply feel better. The best advice I can give for those dealing with something similar is don't overthink it. Let love and genuine care for someone struggling with bipolar or any other disorder be your guide. For someone you love, tell them they are loved, listen to them, make every effort to understand them, be there to console them, and encourage them. In other words, showing them they are loved and believed in might be all that is required.

The first signs of her disorder appeared during the teenage years, as is pretty typical for bipolar disorder. On the surface, her moods and behavior seemed to parallel those of a "rebellious teen." This being the uneducated perspective my wife and I were operating from at the time, let's just say we did not handle this situation with the delicacy required in the early stages. There was lots of yelling, punishments, anger, misunderstandings, resentment, and disrespect, and I think we all felt a little lost. Her acts of defiance became increasingly drastic to the point where we began to suspect something deeper was developing.

My wife and I took her to see a psychologist, and that is where we received the bipolar diagnosis. That visit led to seeing a psychiatrist where my daughter was prescribed different medications for her condition. In our situation, having an understanding did not make things better. In fact, things got worse after receiving the diagnosis. My daughter went through an even darker period. On her bad days, her erratic behavior became more self-destructive and more frequent. She was hospitalized once and had two stays in behavioral facilities. We seemed to be headed toward a dangerous place.

Once again, my wife and I were afraid and unsure, but we knew we had to do something. My wife searched frantically for different psychologists, and I decided to take matters into my own hands. I figured I knew my daughter better than any facility, so if anyone could understand and relate to her, it would be me. So that's what we did. My wife found a wonderful therapist, and I began having regular heart-to-heart conversations with my daughter.

In terms of therapy, I will say this: it is crucial to find the right therapist. Through this process we learned therapy is not one size fits all. Therapists are people too, and if personalities clash, more harm than good could result from the interaction. For us, therapy and deepening our relationship with our child turned out to be the formula for positive progress. As we have learned from earlier chapters in this book, every person is on their own unique journey through life. Knowing my daughter led me to understand why so many problems occurred with the diagnosis, medication, and facilities. My daughter was labeled, and she took it to heart. She felt as though bipolar meant she was crazy or something was wrong with her. Something she and I have in common is we do not particularly like labels for people. Because she was struggling, she accepted the diagnosis as a viable explanation for why she felt the way she did. She took on the "I'm bipolar" mindset.

I made it my mission to help her shed that label and realize bipolar is just a name for fluctuating emotions and does not define her as a person. I asked her, "Since when do you allow people to tell you who you are or what you can be?" I knew from that point of view she would begin to see bipolar disorder in a less debilitating way. Anyone who knows her understands that a command will fall on deaf ears. Once she realized she was in control of who she was, she started to turn the corner out of the darkness and into the light. She understood her value as a person, and she understood she was the only person qualified to set that value by embracing the struggle for control of her mind.

Her diagnosis can't do that. Her mom and I can't do that. Medication can help clear the mind, but it does not establish her value as a person. Because she understands that, she embodies the self-centered perspective perfectly. She constantly strives to keep her mind working for her instead of against her. She focuses relentlessly on her mindset and staying positive because she knows that is best for her disposition. Being in control of herself means she can be in better control of the controllable aspects of her daily life. She no longer takes medication, she has a steady job, she's in a long-term relationship, and she is currently house shopping. From the onset of her diagnosis to where she is today, her progress has been tremendous.

I share this story with you because I have witnessed the power of a reflective approach to navigating life's rocky roads. The paths we take to a destination might differ, but the one thing I believe to be universal is that if we take the time to do what is necessary to present the best possible version of ourselves out in the world, the world would be a better place for everyone. I know my daughter interacts with the world in a better way based on how she feels about herself, and her progress speaks for itself.

◆ ◆ ◆

NAVIGATING ADDICTION

By now we are all aware of the destructive power of our emotions if we allow them to guide our choices without filtering them through our principles. Another biological challenge we face is the possibility of having genes that make us susceptible to addiction.

Addiction has similar effects to allowing our emotions to rage out of control. Both can lead us down a path of executing harmful behaviors that are not in our best interest. I have witnessed the damaging effects of addiction on the individual battling the disease as well as on those around the individual. From irresponsible decision-making to breaking up families to loss of life, addiction is scary and typically brings nothing but hardship.

There are opposing views among the masses when it comes to addiction being a disease or a choice. I, being a strong proponent of the power of the mind, believe most addictions to be a choice that can evolve into a disease. Babies can be born addicted to drugs, unfortunately, but that does not mean that child has to remain on drugs for the rest of their life to survive. Babies do not emerge from the womb looking for the tequila and wagering the crib and all their diapers on the Eagles to cover against the Cowboys. Point being, we are not typically born addicted to the many things in life people become addicted to.

Suffering from addiction results from choosing to experience the effects of drugs or alcohol for the first time—or the euphoria of gambling, skydiving, eating sugar, or scrolling through TikTok or some other social media platform for hours. That may be all it takes for those born with stronger addictive personality genes to become addicted. Ultimately, a choice was made to engage and continue engaging in a behavior that can get out of control. Because I believe this is a choice, I believe the self-centered perspective can be effective in dealing with addiction.

The first order of business is to separate the behavior from the person. We must not use phrases such as "I'm an addict" or "You're an addict," which label the individual negatively, thereby increasing the complexity of the journey to overcome the affliction. On top of the addiction issue, now we also have to navigate lowered self-esteem and self-worth, lengthening the recovery process. I have never attended an AA meeting, but if the representations of the introduction I have seen are accurate, I disagree with its premise. As a self-centered individual, it is up to me to choose how I want to be defined. I would not say, "Hi, my name is Ray, and I'm an alcoholic." Instead, I would say, "Hi, I'm Ray, and I struggle with alcohol abuse." From this perspective, alcohol abuse is something I do, not who I am.

Separating the person from the behavior clarifies that the objective is to battle addiction, not ourselves. Self-efficacy helps us take this stance because we need to believe we are not defined by our deficiencies. Once we believe, by default we acknowledge our value and the need to do what is best for us. With our well-being as motivation, the likelihood of our doing the work it takes to overcome an addiction increases dramatically.

◆ ◆ ◆

NAVIGATING PRESSURE

> No matter how good you are at planning, the pressure never goes away. So I don't fight it. I feed off it. I turn pressure into motivation to do my best.
>
> —**Ben Carson**

A major cause for anxiety in humans is the different types of pressure we feel just living our lives. Pressure comes in three forms: inner, peer, and societal.

♦ INNER PRESSURE

Inner pressure must be examined closely because it is essential to identify the root cause of the pressure we put on ourselves. If we did a deep dive into the reason for elevated stress in pressure situations, I wager most of us would come to a surprising conclusion. The internal pressure we feel actually originates from an external source, typically the situation we are faced with. For example, if we know a presentation to a client at work will be the deciding factor for landing a huge account, we might put pressure on ourselves to make that presentation flawless. If it's not, will we be not only the reason the account went in a different direction but also the source of everyone's disappointment. This is not true inner pressure because the presentation itself and the thought of letting other people down is the actual source of the pressure, not us.

The external source could be the environment we grew up in. If we were raised to prioritize responsibility above all else, that could lead to a life of constant pressure to be perfect parents, to make enough money to pay all the bills on time, to keep the house clean, and to remember to execute all the other constants in our daily lives. That pressure stems from the environment that conditioned our brain to believe that is the right way to live.

The culture of fitting in can also be a source of pressure masquerading as internal. I have talked with family and friends about the pressure they put on themselves to appear as though they have it all together when they are out in public. They bottle up their true feelings and put on a happy face to avoid uncomfortable interactions or judgment. They feel the pressure of "keeping it together" in front of others, but this pressure stems from society and not from within.

Our life experiences shape our way of thinking, and this feels natural because that's how it seems to work for everyone else. The self-centered perspective eliminates external influences as a source of pressure. The best way for the self-centered person to navigate internal pressure is to understand it is not meant to be negative. Pressure that originates from within should be a byproduct of one's own goal setting. When we set personal goals, we also put pressure on ourselves to be accountable for every step of the process. This pressure is designed to be the ultimate motivation for taking action and striving to make our dreams come true—especially when we dream big. Big dreams always meet with some form of resistance, and at times making them happen takes a singular focus and resilience.

Our inner pressure can drive us through adverse situations and strengthen our resilience. We can experience real growth in character by defining our expectations based on what we know about ourselves, without outside influences.

◆ PEER PRESSURE

The most common external pressure we face is peer pressure, which is placed on us by those close to us, such as family, friends, coworkers, or a group of people in a social class we'd like to join. Peer pressure is dangerous because some behaviors we allow ourselves to get talked into are not in our best interest. Young children and teenagers are the most susceptible; those are the prime years for establishing identity and fitting in with a particular group.

The self-centered perspective combats peer pressure by

empowering the notion that individuality is healthier than being a follower. Choosing to be influenced by the wrong people can devastate a person's self-worth. Adults must show young people the value of advocating for themselves and standing for principles that do not waver amid adversity. We positively influence the young by how we conduct ourselves, showing them leadership stems from being confident in and true to our beliefs. That makes us trustworthy and genuine, two qualities worthy of respect.

When we are self-centered, peer pressure can be useful; I believe we should view it as a challenge and an opportunity to self-evaluate. When faced with peer pressure, we can test our convictions, morals, and self-confidence. If we are uncomfortable in the situation, let's think about why. Which area of our character needs to be strengthened if we feel we are succumbing to peer pressure? If we are challenged by friends to participate in an act in which we do not wish to participate but we have a strong desire to "fit in," this is a perfect opportunity to boost our conviction by stating we do not wish to participate. By standing up for our beliefs, we increase our efficacy, strengthening our self-centered perspective.

◆ SOCIETAL PRESSURE

Societal pressure has become much more prevalent with advances in technology. Mainstream media, social media, and the internet are more influential than ever. Information and ideals circulate throughout society, projecting images and scripting narratives of what it means to be successful, intelligent, beautiful, and healthy. Societal pressure elevates wealth, socioeconomic status, and physical attractiveness, creating a culture where people feel better than or less than others. We must remember that the media and society have agendas designed to appeal to the masses. We are individuals! We should not conform our thoughts and behaviors to media propaganda that does not apply to our natural and comfortable physical and emotional states.

Financial wealth is not the only way to have status or be held in high regard by others. Sharing knowledge, being kind, and treating others with respect will garner genuine love. The affinity people have for us is then based on who we are and not what we have. Similarly, physical attractiveness is not the only way to be beautiful. As a society, we seem obsessed with outer beauty. We do drastic things to our bodies to be considered "good looking": surgical reductions, surgical enhancements, Botox, sixty-minute makeup routines, hair coloring to hide the gray, creams for every body part, and magic cream that somehow fights aging. What does anti-aging even mean?! If I want to combat aging, I will do it with good old-fashioned healthy eating and exercise and not with some potion that supposedly makes my wrinkles vanish upon application.

Society presents these options to us, preying on our insecurities as humans and making us feel as though we need these goods and services. The self-centered perspective helps us recognize that surface beauty is fleeting and results from the genetic lottery. All we can do is make the most of what we have, which will be enough to attract the right people.

Think about a person with stunning surface beauty who lacks compassion, lacks intelligence, and is narcissistic and rude. A purely physical relationship might be acceptable in the short term, but in the long run, the beautiful narcissist will be alone with no real connections. On the other hand, think about a person who is short on surface beauty but is compassionate, intelligent, treats everyone as an equal, and is kind beyond belief. This type of person attracts others to their soul. These are the people who find soulmates and spend a lifetime fulfilled by being loved and respected. The self-centered message is that being true to ourselves gives us the best chance to experience genuine relationships and peace of mind, knowing that societal representations of a "good life" will not always apply to our real lives.

♦ ♦ ♦

NAVIGATING SUCCESS

> Success is peace of mind which is a direct result
> of self-satisfaction in knowing you did your best
> to become the best you are capable
> of becoming.
>
> —John Wooden

In most situations, adversity and negativity are the sources of our stress, anxiety, and other unfavorable emotions. These feelings lead us to experience negative life events. For some, success also lies at the root of these events. What kind of a crazy world do we live in where prosperity can be viewed as a hardship? I'll tell you.

Success can become an issue for one of two reasons. It alters either our personality or the personalities of people around us for the worse. The number one measure of success in society is the size of one's bank account. A well-known biblical proverb states, "The love of money is the root of all evil." It has been broadened over time to suggest money itself is the root of all evil, but I could not disagree more with that statement. *People* decide to sacrifice morals and principles to acquire money; therefore, the mindsets and motivations of people are at the root of all evil.

Affluence often comes with an elitist attitude. Success typically brings attention and recognition, so these people act superior to those who have not attained their level of success. They talk down to those they view as less than. They make light of careers they feel are beneath them. They prattle on and on about their accomplishments, their wealth, their belongings, or their exotic vacations.

The successful can lose sight of their humanity and alienate those around them. They get comfortable, and the mindset that propelled them to success is lost, which opens the door for a potential downfall they may not be equipped to manage. Success can lead to reckless behavior, complacency, and an inability to communicate well with others, resulting in being perceived as unlikable or intolerable. This behavior is not reserved for the financially successful. It occurs in people who experience any kind of success. Being famous, having a fancy job title, or parenting successful kids can bring out a similar superiority complex.

When we have success in anything, it is so important to stay humble and not lose the resilience it takes to achieve success. We must keep learning and growing because as human beings we will never be a finished product. If we adopt the perspective of being human above all, we understand our success could be gone in an instant or dissipate over time if we rest on our laurels or after a series of bad decisions, which humans are prone to make. We are one unfortunate event away from being "just like everyone else." This perspective reminds us always to treat people with respect. If we happen to fall, we may need a little help getting back up. But if we manage to offend enough people with our conceit, arrogance, and poor attitude while we're on top, we might not find a single helping hand.

The other side of this scenario is how our success can impact those around us. Even if we are fortunate enough to experience success and self-centered enough to stay grounded and humble, sometimes family, friends, and strangers create difficult circumstances to navigate. They treat us differently than other people, as if we are suddenly more important than we were before our success. People we normally don't have contact with reach out. Those same people may exaggerate the nature of our relationship to suggest we are closer than we are. They do this to elevate their status. To have a relationship with someone successful is the next best thing to having personal success. They feel important by association.

We now have to decipher the intentions of everyone around us. Are these people reaching out because they are genuinely proud of our accomplishments, or do they have ulterior motives that benefit them? If we aren't careful, this special treatment can impact the way we interact with others. Sometimes we feel forced to put up boundaries, distance ourselves from the attention, or act rudely to protect ourselves. Even if our intent is honorable, as in simply trying to protect our privacy, our actions might come off as standoffish, giving the impression we think we are better than others even though that may not be the case. We just have to live with that misunderstanding.

A tip of the cap to all those who have achieved success and fame. I cannot imagine everybody knowing who I am wherever I go, preventing me from living my life. People would want to talk, take pictures, and get autographs when all I want to do is buy some milk at the grocery store and go home. I recognize the appeal of being a celebrity, but I understand the challenges as well. The self-centered perspective would serve us well under these circumstances; we simply have to stay true to our beliefs and not put too much emphasis on how people around us behave. If we live by the pillars of being self-centered, success can be dealt with by staying humble, being accountable to our beliefs, and engaging in behaviors we have chosen that best represent us despite what's going on around us.

◆ ◆ ◆

NAVIGATING RELATIONSHIPS

> Real magic in relationships means an absence of judgment of others.
>
> —Wayne Dyer

As mentioned earlier, life is a series of interactions with other people. Our more personal interactions are considered relationships. The big four in terms of relationships are family, friends, work, and romance. Each type of relationship can enrich or complicate our life, depending on how we nurture it. Even though each type comes with unique challenges and characteristics, the secret to cultivating a healthy relationship in all cases is humility.

It may seem counterintuitive to take a self-centered approach to relationships, but remember: to be self-centered means to have a solid understanding of how situations work. A relationship, by definition, means at least two people are involved. We have no control over the other person in the relationship, so by process of elimination, the only element of the relationship we can control is ourselves. That is right in our wheelhouse.

If we treat the relationship the way we believe the relationship needs to be treated, we're doing all we can. People tend to mimic each other, so in approaching a relationship or potential relationship with humility and an open mind, we encourage a similar approach from another. But we never know how someone might respond to our attempts to foster positive relations. Take courting, for example. Out there on the dating scene, we cannot know with certainty that our actions will lead to successful dates. If the person we wish to establish a good relationship with does not wish to have a relationship with us, then I'm afraid that event lands in the "elements out of our control" category. The only option at this point is to lean on our resilience and not give up after a single rejection if we feel a connection with this person. It is important, however, to recognize the thin line between persistence and stalker-type behavior; learn when to throw in the towel.

Not everyone will be interested in growing a relationship with us. We have much better odds of developing a healthy relationship with people we spend a substantial amount of time with. As I mentioned at the start of this section, the approach for establishing strong relationships is essentially the same for each type. I will further discuss romantic relationships to give an example for cultivating an unbreakable bond between romantic partners that applies to every kind of relationship.

I have been happily married for thirteen years. My wife is my soulmate, and she enhances my quality of life like nothing else can.

Despite our strong connection, early on in our marriage, we disagreed about certain things, and we would argue. Nothing too crazy, but there was yelling at times. At other times, it was the silent treatment. There may have been a tossed chair here, a broken TV remote there, but we were arguing, and tempers ran hot, so "these things happen." That was my socially acceptable justification. Conventional wisdom suggests conflict is inevitable for long-term romantic partners, but after my baptism in 2013, I began questioning my actions during our disagreements.

My wife has a fiery side. Once unleashed, things can go sideways quickly. I swear, she used to look for any little reason to pick a fight. It didn't have to make sense! I had become so accustomed to allowing my emotions to dictate my actions in these situations that it never dawned on me that I had a choice in participating in these arguments. As I began transforming my character and deciding what kind of person I wanted to be, I realized this included deciding what kind of husband I wanted to be. That's when the metaphorical light bulb turned on. I thought about what's most important to me. There is no one I love, respect, and cherish more than my wife. Why would I ever treat someone I hold in the highest possible regard poorly? What kind of husband would do that? How does that approach communicate love and respect? Here's a shocking revelation: it doesn't!

I realized if I was acting that way, I wasn't being true to my feelings and what matters most. Right then and there, I chose to never argue with my wife again.

My wife and I have very different temperaments. She is a bit high strung, and I don't think I even have strings. The next time she got upset and wanted to fight, I simply refused to engage. Instead of arguing, I replied with something like this:

"I have far too much love and admiration for you to fight with you. I have absolutely no desire to treat you with anything other than the respect you've earned over the course of our relationship. When we treat each other as though there is no love present, we disrespect our marriage, but if yelling at me will make you genuinely feel better and get back to enjoying your life, then I'm happy to sit here and allow you to vent.

"However, if that's not going to make you feel better, why even go down that road? Let's skip the negativity and just work on the solution to our disagreement like two people in love who care about each other's feelings and want nothing but good things for each other."

This interaction occurred years ago, so this is paraphrased, but the general message is accurate. Since that day, my wife and I haven't had one fight. Choosing to conduct ourselves without the influence of emotions can positively impact our quality of life.

The same principles apply to family and friend relationships. Hopefully when dealing with family and close friends, the love and respect in those connections has more value than hostile, temporary emotions that pop up during a disagreement. If we hold these people in high esteem, we can better manage our negative emotions and navigate the nonsense peacefully. With work relationships, the matter is one of respect and personal professionalism. We must choose to be a coworker who is solution based, with no need for office politics, gossip, or jealousy. If we stay calm and rational in all interactions, the relationship can always be productive.

The beauty of only controlling ourselves in a relationship is that our feelings, actions, and what we want out of a relationship don't have to be contingent on the other person's feelings, actions, and view of the relationship. So often I hear people complaining about the inequities of their relationships. "I do this, that, and the other, and they only do that. It's not fair!" "I do so much for them, and they aren't even grateful. Screw them!" "Why should I be the only one going out of my way to nurture this relationship? It should be fifty-fifty. If they aren't willing to meet me halfway, then I guess the relationship is a bust." These perspectives are not necessarily wrong, but they place too much emphasis on external forces, and we lose our humility when we think this way.

The self-centered perspective focuses solely on how we feel and what we want without the interference of negative emotions, other people's behavior, or unjustified expectations. I will use my relationship with my wife as an example again. I do not do things for my wife for gratitude or recognition or the expectation that what I've done will be reciprocated. The foundation of my relationship is not a favor for a favor. I do things for my wife because I love her. I appreciate her, I want to see her smile, and I want to see her happy. Most importantly, I do things for her because I want to. There are no ulterior motives. If there are times in our relationship I have to go 80 percent to her 20, I'll do it without hesitation because I know that's what she needs. I feel truly blessed that she will go 100 to my 0 (which is the more likely scenario), but I do not expect that of her. She will do that because that's how much she cares about me, not to pay me back for something I have done for her in the past.

We must temper our expectations in relationships because in setting expectations, we assert that other people should view the situation similar to how we are viewing it. Sometimes the feeling of inequity is a simple misunderstanding.

A popular book written by Gary Chapman about love languages stresses the different ways people express their affection for one another. *The 5 Love Languages: The Secret to Love that Lasts* is a great resource for relationships. One simple yet very important aspect to understand is that people are different. We have differing strengths and weaknesses, and what we demand of others in a relationship might not be their strong suit. Remember, the self-centered perspective directs us to be humble and understand we all have flaws. Maybe the person we are trying to have a good relationship with is not intentionally trying to make us feel bad or unimportant. Maybe they're just not good at expressing themselves in the method we prefer.

We must communicate to gain understanding. Even if we have to do 90 percent of the work to someone else's 10 percent, it will be worth it; ultimately, that work will benefit us most of all.

CHAPTER 13

BE SELF-CENTERED

Let the improvement of yourself keep you so busy that you have no time to criticize others.

—Roy T. Bennett

You have the key to unlock whatever quality of life you want. Making the effort to understand the challenges life presents gives you a much greater chance to craft effective game plans to overcome those challenges. The stars in your unique game plan are your DNA, your perception, your understanding, and your choices. These elements will guide you to the self-centered perspective.

Live your life with the purpose of developing your mind to be strong enough to withstand the inevitable hits you must endure. By becoming a self-centered individual, you will be **humble** in your approach to life. You will be understanding, sympathetic, encouraging, and kind. You will treat others with respect, and you will not accept disrespect from anyone regardless of status.

You will have high **efficacy**. You will always believe in your worth as a member of humanity and your ability to learn and grow. You will be confident in who you are and stand behind the principles by which you live without fear of judgment or not fitting in or the need for external approval.

You will be **accountable** to yourself above all others. Create a high standard for your character and make every effort to personify that standard as you interact with the world. Routinely assess yourself and make the necessary adjustments when you are not living up to your principles. If you see yourself as a finished product, you sabotage your potential to evolve your character.

You will be **resilient**. Negativity, adversity, and tragic life experiences will be viewed as temporary. They will get you down. They will hurt—momentarily. That is the nature of emotions, and of life experiences. They must come to an end. You decide the duration of your sadness, anger, or pain. Don't let your emotions dictate your actions. Take action to balance out your emotions.

You will be **trustworthy**. Always be honest with yourself. That is the only way to grow as a person. Say what you mean, mean what you say, and support your words with actions. As a person who can be trusted, you earn respect while making the world a safer place. You enhance the quality of life for yourself and all those around you. By living your life with HEART, you are trying to put the best version of yourself on display. You will find strength where there used to be stress, clarity in the chaos, and fortitude in the face of misfortune. Life is as straightforward or as complicated as you make it.

Stop mindlessly following trends and conforming to social norms. Stop accepting labels that seek to define you as a person. Stop allowing your emotions to treat you like a puppet, stringing you along, telling you how to feel and how to behave. Only you can determine who you want to be and how you want to carry yourself. You have a choice! Your mind is one of the world's greatest marvels. Please use its power to aid you on your quest to become self-motivated and self-sustaining. Most importantly, see the quality of your life improve, starting today, by seizing control of your mind and choosing to become **self-centered!**

EPILOGUE

You already have everything you need to replace the negative emotions you experience, like stress, anxiety, sadness, and anger, with positive emotions like serenity, confidence, appreciation, and joy. You have been walking around with the master key to a higher quality of life hidden in your mind. That key is your power to choose how to conduct yourself and the perspective with which you interact with the world.

An introspective approach to life mitigates many of the negative experiences you are bound to encounter over the span of a lifetime. The self-centered perspective spawned the five principal pillars, the character traits that will help you take control of your mind and raise your emotional awareness. The five traits, in the form of an acronym, spell out the word "heart." HEART represents a way of living that increases personal understanding, confidence, and quality of life. This set of core traits—humility, efficacy, accountability, resilience, and trust—will help you successfully navigate life's ups and downs. These traits provide the clarity you need when setting goals for your success or facing the inevitable adversities you will encounter simply because you are human.

The purpose of the book is to remind you that you have a choice in your daily disposition. No external force or emotions should control how you behave. I want to see a world where everyone chooses to walk the high road—where the environment is never toxic, the scenery is beautiful, and the company is always pleasant.

I am a man of faith, family, and specific principles. I have a bachelor of science degree in psychology, which I only mention to illustrate my genuine passion for the mind, which I believe is the greatest gift to humanity. This is my first published book, my attempt to reach different people and encourage them to advocate for themselves unconditionally. My passion for higher quality living, my desire to help others achieve a higher quality of living, and my ability to mitigate my negative behaviors with the power of my mind motivates me to help as many people as possible to feel more blessed than stressed.

As for my part in that endeavor, I provide life coaching services via my website. I know everyone may not be able to afford professional counseling. If you need advice, emotional support, or just someone to talk to, join the HEART community, and every effort will be made to help you feel better and to feel like you are in control of your destiny. I genuinely care for the well-being of all my brothers and sisters, and I am not looking to profit from the misery of others. I want to see you living with a sustainable, healthy life perspective and the confidence to understand that everything you need exists within you, and, eventually, you might not need therapy or counseling. You will know that your authentic self is more than enough to survive and thrive in this world.

◆ ◆ ◆

THE LOGO

The logo is meant to represent who you are. The heart represents the courage it takes to love, show compassion, and advocate for yourself unconditionally 100 percent of the time. The diamond, the hardest material on earth, represents the unwavering commitment to living the HEART way of life as your authentic self without needing external validation or conforming to social norms. It is the most vital commitment you will ever make, and just as natural diamonds are unique, so are we as humans. If you are the type of person who believes in always being yourself, this logo represents you perfectly.

◆ ◆ ◆

POEMS

As we live our lives, happiness often seems like it resides at the top of a mountain made of ice, and all we have to help us reach it is a pair of heavily used ice skates. Metaphorically, our life represents the process of scaling that mountain.

If you have ever attempted ice-skating uphill, you know it is a challenge, to say the least—very similar to living our life. In fact, the degree of difficulty can be so high for some that it does not seem worth the struggle. My heart aches for those who lose the will to climb at some point during the ascent. If you or someone you know struggles to find a purpose for living, please know there are people out there who genuinely care for your health and well-being. You are not alone. If you feel lonely and are unable to find someone to be there for you in a time of need, please know that a relationship with yourself can be very helpful.

Myself and the guy in the mirror have become pretty tight over the years. That reflection looking back at me knows and understands everything I feel and go through. A little understanding can go a long way in a relationship with yourself and others. Life is extremely difficult at times, but we are equipped with free will and the power to choose whichever disposition we desire. Everyone has value and capability. Sometimes we need a reminder of that, and our reflection, which always has our back, is perfect for slipping us that memo when we need it.

My wife enjoys poetry, and it has become a method by which I express my thoughts and feelings, so I've included a couple of poems to help process life's hardships and to stress the importance of advocating for yourself by having a good relationship with yourself. There is a special one for my wife as an expression of how much better she makes my life.

◆ ◆ ◆

AN UNCONDITIONAL RELATIONSHIP

Solitude can be the bane of a human.
Loneliness engulfs the heart with sorrow.
With desperation and dark thoughts loomin',
There is little yearning to see tomorrow,

To feel like a burden or societal outcast.
If life were to cease, all pain left behind,
The forlorn mindset you may outlast.
By living with HEART, you revitalize the mind.

Establish love in your heart with someone there 'til the end
Who will not judge or put anything above you.
Your reflection, your soulmate—if you just let it in,
It is someone to love; someone to love you.

Life can be arduous, a labyrinthine test.
With your HEART as your guide, you will live and be blessed.

THE BEST RELATIONSHIP

Unconditional love is a good place to start
Never underestimate the power of the heart
Diligence in considering all of the facts
Evolutionary is one who puts thought before acts
Rising above external irrelevance
Showing mastery of emotional intelligence
Taboo are thoughts that are self-serving
Awareness is the path to follow without swerving
No judgment is levied, just open minds
Distinguishing circumstances of all kinds
Improving relationships is the name of the game
Nobody's fault, no assessment of blame
God shows forgiveness, and we do the same.

A MESSAGE TO MY WIFE

My heart is completely yours
You brighten my day with a slight touch
Because of you, our relationship soars
Everyday a blessing to love so much
An angel disguised in mortal attire
Unique qualities separate from the masses
Too many fine traits for me to admire
Infinite is my love as time passes
Future days with you bring me joy
Unlike any other pleasure
Love & trust travel in a convoy
With a respect too powerful to measure
Inspired is how you make me feel
Fully committed to only you
Enchanted dreams made to be real
Living this heaven reservation for two
Impossible some say was our connection
No believers, but we had each other
Deciding love was worth facing imperfection
Since I met you, there will never be another
Always know deep in your heart
You are my lighthouse, my guiding light
Anchoring our souls even if apart
Never regret and never lose sight
Nothing and nobody can say we weren't right.

ACKNOWLEDGMENTS

Writing a book is one of the most challenging exercises I have ever undertaken. I have an incredible amount of respect for those who dedicate their lives to crafting words to uplift, inform, and entertain. A tip of the cap to all authors, songwriters, and screenplay writers. Your talents and dedication to vocabulary and transforming the fluent structure of words into sentences and art are not lost on me. Thank you for your efforts.

As much appreciation as I have gained for those who write, I am even more appreciative of the people who helped make this dream of mine come true. My family is an incredible support system. Without them, not only would this book not exist, but I would certainly not be the person I am. I don't want to go overboard and share every remarkable trait the members of my inner circle possess, but I do want them and you to understand how much I cherish having them in my life.

To my wife, my number one supporter/critic, my truest friend, and my better half: You are an astonishing woman who has it all—brains, beauty, selflessness to a fault, and the toughest work ethic in the business of heading a household. You are the ultimate caretaker of the kids and me in every way, and you bring a joy to my life that can only be compared to what eternal life in heaven must be like. Thank you, Lindsay, my amazing bride. I could not have done this without your support and unwavering belief in me.

To my parents: Without the unconditional love and support I received from you in absolutely everything I've ever done, I don't know if I would have developed the confidence and courage to always be me. Thank you, Raymond and Annie, for arming me with a solid foundation of ethics and a moral compass that cannot be interfered with by even the most powerful magnet.

To my sister: Rarely does an older brother look up to a younger sister, but that is the case for me. You are the epitome of confidence and style. Your sense of humor brings me joy daily, and siblings don't come any better than you. The way you carry yourself pushes me to be better. Tamika Rochele (UNM Basketball Hall of Famer), I can't thank you enough for that.

To my children: You guys are my greatest source of pride. You bring me so much happiness and so much fulfillment just being who you are. Each of you in your own unique way inspires me to be the best version of myself every day. Denzel, Lexi-Rayn, Terayah, Treydan, and Nya, thank you all for enriching my life and providing me with the greatest gift and purpose on earth: being your father.

To my mother-in-law: You were the spark that lit the flame for embarking on this journey of writing a book. The love and care you've shown me over the years have been a comfort for my well-being, and I appreciate it greatly. Thank you, Lois, for convincing me to open my mind. It changed my life path.

www.ingramcontent.com/pod-product-compliance
Lightning Source LLC
LaVergne TN
LVHW041606070526
838199LV00052B/3005